THE DEMAND FOR IMPORTS AND EXPORTS IN THE
WORLD ECONOMY

to the memory of
    Mildred Sawyer-Bradley and Luise Scudder

The Demand for Imports and Exports in the World Economy

W. CHARLES SAWYER
University of Southern Mississippi

RICHARD L. SPRINKLE
University of Texas at El Paso

Routledge
Taylor & Francis Group

LONDON AND NEW YORK

First published 1999 by Ashgate Publishing

Reissued 2018 by Routledge
2 Park Square, Milton Park, Abingdon, Oxon, OX14 4RN
711 Third Avenue, New York, NY 10017, USA

Routledge is an imprint of the Taylor & Francis Group, an informa business

Publisher's Note
The publisher has gone to great lengths to ensure the quality of this reprint but points out that some imperfections in the original copies may be apparent.

Disclaimer
The publisher has made every effort to trace copyright holders and welcomes correspondence from those they have been unable to contact.

A Library of Congress record exists under LC control number: 99072975

ISBN 13: 978-1-138-34964-3 (hbk)
ISBN 13: 978-0-429-43626-0 (ebk)

Contents

List of Tables

1 Introduction

One of the oldest areas of empirical analysis in international economics is the examination and estimation of income and price elasticities of the demand for imports and exports. Estimates of the response of imports and exports to changes in these variables are important for several reasons. The income elasticity of the demand for imports and exports is of interest to researchers and policy makers in that these estimates describe how imports or exports respond to changes in domestic (foreign) economic activity (GDP).

Analogously, price elasticities are important in describing how trade flows between countries respond to changes in domestic prices relative to foreign prices. These price elasticities become critical variables when policies related to multilateral tariff reductions are negotiated under the auspices of GATT/WTO, and when bilateral tariff reductions are negotiated under various regional free-trade area agreements. In addition, these price elasticities are critical in estimating the effects of preferential tariff reductions such as the Generalized System of Preferences (GSP) and the Caribbean Basin Initiative (CBI).

Further, in a world of floating exchange rates, the elasticity of trade flows in response to changes in the exchange rate is of obvious interest. Finally, these elasticities and the impact of international trade are becoming of increasing importance the world economy. Imports and exports as a percentage of world output has been increasing for decades and shows no signs of abating.

Orcutt's (1950) seminal paper in this area has been followed by literally hundreds of studies presenting estimates of income and price elasticities for various countries.   For researchers using these elasticities, the sheer volume of the literature presents both advantages and challenges. The advantage is that in many cases relevant elasticities for imports and exports have been published for a wide range of countries, and/or products. The difficulty has been that the volume of the literature has grown so large that finding empirical estimates which best fit the purpose at hand can be a rather tedious process. The solution in many cases has been to rely on two previously published surveys of the import and export demand literature.

The most frequently cited surveys covering elasticities for international trade are by Stern, Francis, and Schumacher (1976) and Goldstein and Khan (1985). Both surveys are among the most widely cited pieces in international trade. Since 1977 these two surveys have been cited nearly 250 times. The former survey is extensive but now suffers from the fact that the elasticities reported are dated. The latter survey also is used frequently as a source of income and price elasticity estimates. However, this work focuses more on data and econometric estimation issues involved in the estimation of import and export demand elasticities rather than surveying the empirical estimates. While this paper is more recent than the previous survey, the results reported are now at best over fifteen years old.

The purpose of this volume is to update the aforementioned surveys.   More specifically, this survey reviews the literature on empirical estimates of the income and price elasticities of demand for imports and exports by country which have been published since 1976. This information should be of interest to researchers and policy markers needing a convenient source for estimates. In total, we provide 979 estimates of import and export demand elasticities covering 82 countries. The estimates are presented in a relatively easy-to-use format.   Finally, the estimates may also be useful in providing researchers a convenient way to look both at what is currently known and where there are gaps in the literature.

The next chapter of this volume provides a discussion of some of the issues involved in the estimation of the income and price elasticities of the demand for imports and exports. In addition, this chapter contains a discussion of the evolution of the literature over the last 20 years. Chapter 3 contains the empirical estimates from 1976 to date for the demand for imports by country. Chapter 4 contains like estimates for the demand for exports by country. The final chapter contains a summary and concludes with what is known concerning import and export demand elasticities.

2 Econometric Estimation of Trade Elasticities

The econometric modeling of aggregate trade flows has a long history in the economic and applied econometric literature. Beginning in the late 1950s with Cheng (1959), a number of important surveys have been published including Leamer and Stern (1970), Magee (1975), Stern et al. (1976) and Goldstein and Khan (1985). One of the reasons for the important amount of published studies is certainly the fact that the underlying theoretical economic framework for the determination of prices and trade volumes is reasonably straightforward and familiar from standard consumer demand or production theory. In addition, the effectiveness of international trade policies is dependent on the size of the price and income effects on trade flows. As such, policy makers have an important interest in reliable estimates of these parameters.

Although the nature of the goods being traded (homogeneous commodities versus differentiated goods); the end-use of the commodity (for final consumption versus an intermediate good); and the geographical distribution of trade are factors which are important in modeling disaggregated trade flows, we restrict our attention to total aggregate trade flows so that the basic underlying economic theory can remain relatively familiar. Traditionally, the basic question of whether imports and exports are perfect substitutes or imperfect substitutes for domestically produced goods has been often debated (see Leamer and Stern (1970), Goldstein and Khan (1985)). Since intra-industry trade is usually observed between countries, i.e., a country both imports and exports the same commodity, an imperfect substitutes model is the mainstay of empirical work on modeling trade flows.

The imperfect substitutes model (for more detail, see Goldstein and Khan (1985)) is briefly described below for both imports and exports of a country.

The Imperfect Substitutes Model for Imports

For simplicity, consider a country i's imports from the rest of the world. The demand for imports by country i from the rest of the world can be represented as follows:

$$M_i^D \quad = \quad f(Y_i, PM_i, PD_i) \tag{2.1}$$

Where M_i^D denotes the quantity of country i's imports demanded; Y_i denotes the level of money income in country i; PM_i denotes the domestic currency price paid by importers in country i; and PD_i denotes the price of all domestically produced goods within county i. In addition, the domestic currency price paid by importers in country i can be expressed as follows:

$$PM_i \quad = \quad PM_i^*(1+T_i)/XR \tag{2.2}$$

Where PM_i^* denotes the foreign currency price of country i's imports (the price of the rest of the world's exports); T_i denotes the proportional tariff of country i; and XR is the exchange rate defined as units of country i's currency per unit of the rest of the world's currency.

The supply of imports from the rest of the world to country i can be represented as:

$$M_i^S \quad = \quad g(PM_i^*(1 + S^*), PD^*) \tag{2.3}$$

Where S^* denotes the proportional subsidy rate by the rest of the world on exports to country i, and PD^* denotes the foreign currency price of all domestically produced goods in the rest of the world. For notational convenience we have used a simple two country framework which implies symmetry between the demand for imports and the supply of imports such that:

$$M_i^D \quad = \quad M_i^S \tag{2.4}$$

The main characteristics of the imperfect substitutes model for imports can be summarized as follows. In accordance with conventional demand theory, the consuming country is postulated to maximize utility subject to a budget constraint. The resulting demand function for imports thus represents the quantity demanded as a function of the level of money income in country i; the imported good's own price; and the price of domestic substitutes. For aggregate imports the possibility of inferior goods is typically excluded, so the income elasticity f_Y is assumed to be positive. In addition, for aggregate imports the possibility of domestic complements for imports is also excluded, so that the cross-price elasticity, f_{PD} is assumed to be positive and the own-price elasticity of demand f_{PM} is of course expected to be negative.

In addition, most researchers assume that the importing country has no money illusion, so that doubling all prices and money income results in no change in the demand for imports, i.e., $f_Y + f_{PD} + f_{PM} = 0$. As such, this homogeneity assumption is normally expressed by dividing the right hand side of the demand function by PD_i so that the demand function becomes:

$$M_i^D \quad = \quad f(Y_i/PD_i, \ PM_i/PD_i) \tag{2.5}$$

The specification of the supply equation indicates that the quantity supplied is a positive function of the own price and a negative function of the price of domestically produced goods in the exporting country. Imposition of homogeneity on the supply function is equivalent to the restriction that $-g_{PM} = g_{PD^*}$. Even though the theory of export supply to the importing country is still very much contested and is currently an unresolved subject in empirical trade work, the basic premise underlying the supply function is that the supply of exports to the importing country will increase with the profitability of producing and selling exports.

The advantage of presenting both the supply and demand for imports in the imperfect substitutes model is to make it clear that the relationship between quantities and price is, at least in theory, simultaneous. Despite this fundamental point, the majority of the empirical studies on import trade have addressed the supply side of the market only by assumption. Specifically, the prevailing practice has been to assume that the supply function is infinitely elastic, i.e., $g_{PM} = \infty$. The great allure of such an assumption is that it permits satisfactory estimation of the import demand function by single-equation methods. In this formulation, the price of imports, PM_i, is viewed as exogenous.

Lastly, the equilibrium characteristics underlying the imperfect substitutes model are worth noting. The implicit assumption represented in the equilibrium condition is that prices move to equate supply and demand in each time period. This assumption however appears to be inconsistent with the recent view of imperfectly competitive markets, where adjusting prices is not costless, especially when one allows for output costs, costs arising from changing inventories, and other menu costs. As a result, there are several alternatives to deal with the non-market clearing property of the model. First, one can retain this property if non-price rationing variables are included in both the demand and supply equations so that price changes are not the only source of market clearing. Second, one can assume that the observed import quantities and prices are in disequilibrium, and then model the adjustment process. This alternative results in a dynamic model of aggregate imports.

The Imperfect Substitutes Model for Exports

In the case of country i's exports to the rest of the world (i.e., the rest of the world imports) the imperfect substitutes model is very similar. The demand for exports by the rest of the world from country i can be represented as follows:

$$X_i^D = f(YF, PX_i, PD_i) \tag{2.6}$$

Where X_i^D denotes the quantity of country i's exports demanded by the rest of the world; YF denotes the level of money income in the rest of the world; PX_i denotes the domestic currency price received by country i for its exports to the rest of the world; and PD_i denotes the price of all domestically produced goods in the rest of the world. In addition, the foreign currency price paid by importers in the rest of the world (i.e., the foreign currency price of country i's exports) can be expressed as follows:

$$PX_i^* = PX_i(1+T_i^*)XR \tag{2.7}$$

Where PX_i^* denotes the foreign currency price of country i's exports (the price of the rest of the world's imports); XR is the exchange rate defined as units of country i's currency per unit of the rest of the world's currency; and T_i^* denotes the proportional tariff of the rest of the world.

The supply of imports from country i to the rest of the world can be represented as:

$$X_i^S = g(PX_i(1 + S_i), PD_i^*) \tag{2.8}$$

Where S^* denotes the proportional subsidy rate by the rest of the world on exports to country i and PD^* denotes the foreign currency price of all domestically produced goods in the rest of the world. For notational convenience we have used a simple two country framework which implies symmetry between the demand for exports and the supply of exports such that:

$$X_i^D = X_i^S \tag{2.9}$$

The main characteristics of the imperfect substitutes model for exports are similar to those for imports and can be summarized as follows. In accordance with conventional demand theory, the consuming country is postulated to maximize utility subject to a budget constraint. The resulting demand function for exports thus represents the quantity demanded as a function of the level of money income in the foreign country; the exported good's own price; and the price of foreign domestic substitutes. For aggregate exports the possibility of inferior goods is typically excluded, so the income elasticity f_{Y*} is assumed to be positive. In addition, for aggregate exports the possibility of domestic complements for exports is also excluded, so that the cross-price elasticity, f_{PD*} is assumed to be positive and the own-price elasticity of demand f_{PX} is of course expected to be negative.

In addition, most researchers assume that the importing country has no money illusion, so that doubling all prices and money income results in no change in the demand for imports, i.e., $f_{Y*} + f_{PD*} + f_{PX} = 0$. As such, this homogeneity assumption is normally expressed by dividing the right hand side of the demand function by $PD*_i$ so that the demand function becomes:

$$X_i^D \quad = \quad f(YF_i/PD_i, PX_i/PD_i) \qquad (2.10)$$

The specification of the supply equation indicates that the quantity supplied is a positive function of the own price and a negative function of the price of domestically produced goods in the exporting country. Imposition of homogeneity on the supply function is equivalent to the restriction that $-g_{PX} = g_{PD}$. Much like imports, the theory of export supply to the importing country is still very much contested. However, the basic premise underlying the supply function is that the supply of exports to the importing country will increase with the profitability of producing and selling exports.

The advantage of presenting both the supply and demand for imports in the imperfect substitutes model is to make it clear that the relationship between quantities and price is, at least in theory, simultaneous. Despite this fundamental point, the majority of the empirical studies on export trade have addressed the supply side of the market only by assumption. Specifically, the prevailing practice has been to assume that the supply function is infinitely elastic, i.e., $g_{PX} = \infty$. The great allure of such an assumption is that it permits satisfactory estimation of the export demand function by single-equation methods. In this formulation, the price of exports, PX_i, is viewed as exogenous.

Lastly, the equilibrium characteristics underlying the imperfect substitutes model for exports are worth noting. Again, the implicit assumption represented in the equilibrium condition is that prices move to equate supply and demand in each time period. This assumption however appears to be inconsistent with the recent view of imperfectly competitive markets, where adjusting prices is not costless, especially when one allows for output costs; costs arising from changing inventories; and other menu costs. As a result, there are several alternatives to deal with the non-market clearing property of the model. First, one can retain this property if non-price rationing variables are included in both the demand and supply equations so that price changes are not the only source of market clearing. Second, one can assume that the observed export quantities and prices are in disequilibrium, and then model the adjustment process. This alternative results in a dynamic model of aggregate exports.

As we expand the two-country model to an n-country world, the symmetry between the demand for imports and exports disappears. This occurs in part because a country's total imports face competition only from domestic producers, and a country's total exports face competition not only from domestic producers in the foreign importing country but also from third country exports to the importing country. As a result, many export demand equations assume that the dominant relative price competition is between exports from different countries and not price competition between exports of one country and foreign domestic production. Under this assumption the relative-price term that is used in the export demand equation is the ratio of the export price of country i to the export price of other third countries (PX_o) denominated in the same currency, i.e., $PX_i / PX_o XR$. As such, the demand for exports becomes

$$X_i^D \quad = \quad f(YF_i/PD_i, PX_i/PX_o XR) \qquad (2.11)$$

Econometric Issues in Trade Modeling

Since the early empirical studies of trade relations, most researchers have been aware of the statistical problems associated with the econometric modeling of aggregate trade flows. This is mainly due to the seminal paper by Orcutt (1950) who stressed the potential problems underlying single-equation estimation of models like the imperfect substitutes model. Consequently, subsequent researchers have tried to provide better estimates so that they would not be subject to this critique. This has become known as the Orcuttization of empirical trade modeling. The empirical relevance of the points raised by Orcutt (1950) has been extensively analyzed over the past several decades. Both Magee (1975) and Goldstein and Khan (1985) provide an excellent summary of the analysis, and we will not discuss the analysis in detail. Since the mid-1970s the literature has evolved around a succession of issues relating to how these elasticities are used. In addition, the literature has addressed more technical econometric issues which have mirrored the development of time-series econometrics in general.

Prior to the publication of the paper by Murray and Ginman (1976), import demand was always estimated in a price-ratio specification. To a large extent this was done to avoid the multicollinearity usually found between the different price variables used in the estimation. This specification, while convenient, has several drawbacks. First, the specification requires that the demand function is homogeneous in prices. This restriction on the demand function requires that the effects of domestic and imported price changes have the same impact on the quantity imported by a country. Murray and Ginman (1976) presented evidence that the U.S. import demand function may not be homogeneous and should more properly be estimated in split-price form. This issue of homogeneity has not been completely resolved in the literature. As a result, one should view price-ratio estimates with some caution unless the estimated function has been subjected to a specification test. Given the estimates presented in Chapters 3 and 4, it would appear that for many countries the demand functions may not be homogeneous. If this is the case, then aside from the homogeneity problem, using a single price elasticity in empirical analysis of trade flows may yield somewhat inappropriate results.

Starting in the late 1970s, the literature began moving to the estimation of import and export demand using specifications involving some lagged response of trade flows to changes in the independent variables. The idea is that trade flows do not respond instantaneously to changes in income and especially to changes in relative prices and exchange rates. The estimation procedure involved the estimation of some form of polynomial lag structure which allows the effects of changes in the independent variable to build up, peak, and then decline over time. The two most widely cited papers in this regard are Wilson and Tackas (1979) and Stern, Baum and Greene (1979). These estimates are particularly interesting because there appears to be substantial differences in how trade flows respond to changes in income as opposed to changes in relative prices. Among the various components of relative prices, a conventional wisdom has developed that trade flows respond sluggishly in particular to changes in the exchange rate (i.e., hysteresis). For example, see Baldwin (1988) or Dixit (1989). However, a persistent problem is that the theory is vague concerning the specifics of the lags. This leads to virtually allowing the data to determine the specifics such as the degree of the polynomial and the length of the lags. For both functions, the lag on the income term appears to be less than two quarters. With respect to the import demand function, the lags on the relative price variables may take ten to twelve quarters to affect imports. The lags on the relative price terms for the export demand function are much shorter.

Starting in the late 1970s, rapid advances in time-series econometrics led the literature in this area into what was essentially a reconsideration of the previously published literature. The development of tests for the structural stability of estimated regressions led to a number of papers beginning with Stern, Baum, and Greene (1979) which considered the structural stability of estimated import and export demand equations. Likewise, the development of specification tests quickly spread into the import demand literature. An influential paper by Thursby and Thursby (1984) led to the incorporation of tests for specification error in a number of subsequent papers. The development of the concept of cointegration (and related concepts) has been an important issue in this literature for the last several years. Fortunately it appears that at least with respect to cointegration, the estimated relationships seem to be valid. For a thorough discussion of cointegration see Carone (1996). As such, the later estimates are better in two senses. First, they use more recent data. Second, the later estimates in most cases have incorporated at least some of the newer issues that have been raised in time-series econometrics. However, one should keep in mind when viewing the tables in the next two chapters that few of the papers cover all of the issues raised in the econometric literature.

3 The Demand for Imports

Before considering the elasticities contained in Tables 3.1 through 3.3, some explanatory notes concerning what is covered and not covered is in order. The estimates begin with studies published from roughly 1976 to the most recently available estimates. The survey by Stern, Francis, and Schumacher (1976) covers studies published through 1975. Thus, 1976 is a convenient point of departure. Our discussion of the estimation of import demand elasticities in Chapter 2 implies that some types of import demand elasticities are not presented in the following tables. As we indicated in that chapter, the standard formulation for estimating import demand can be expressed in one of three equations.

The traditional approach to estimating the demand for imports relates changes in the quantity of imports (M) to changes in income and relative prices.

$$M = f(\overset{+}{Y}, \overset{-}{PM/PD}) \qquad (3.1)$$

The algebraic signs above the variables indicate the expected signs of the first partial derivative of the function with respect to each of the arguments. The variables are domestic income (Y) usually expressed as real GDP or real GNP; the price of imports (PM) usually an import unit value index; and domestic prices (PD) usually expressed as the wholesale price index.

15

The second approach to estimating the demand for imports employs a split-price specification as opposed to the price ratio contained in equation 3.1. This formulation relates changes in the quantity of imports (M) to changes in income and prices separately.

$$\overset{+\quad-\quad+}{M \;=\; f(Y, PM, PD)} \tag{3.2}$$

Where the variables are defined as above. This specification has the advantage of allowing differential responses in import volumes to changes in international prices (PM) versus domestic prices (PD). This could be critical in analyzing changes in imports resulting from changes in exchange rates or domestic trade barriers where the price changes would be solely in the imported price.

A final formulation of the demand for imports involves the decomposition of the imported price into changes in foreign prices (PM) and changes in the exchange rate (XR). The specification of the demand for imports can be represented by:

$$\overset{+\quad-\quad+\quad-/+}{M \;=\; f(Y, PM, PD, XR)} \tag{3.3}$$

Where PM in this formulation represents the price of imports expressed in foreign currency separate from the exchange rate, XR. The advantage of this specification is that it allows one to view how imports respond to changes in the exchange rate as a separate issue. The algebraic sign associated with XR depends on the way the exchange rate is defined. The exchange rate variable will be negative if the exchange rate is defined in terms of local currency per unit of foreign currency, and positive if defined in terms of foreign currency per unit of domestic currency.

Equations 3.1 through 3.3 represent the "standard" view of these relationships, however, there are two other approaches to estimating the demand for imports which we do not consider and are not included in the following tables. First, the production function approach to import demand is not covered. This approach is a quantitatively small part of the literature. In addition, the estimated elasticities are not easily comparable to the traditional estimation procedures. For an extensive survey and discussion of this approach see Kohli (1991). Second, studies employing the Armington approach to estimating import demand have not been reported. This approach has been extensively used in the area of agricultural economics. For a recent discussion of this approach see Shiells and Reinert (1993). Third, several of the estimated import demand functions contained in the following tables do not use these standard views. In several cases, the import demand equation has been estimated without price variables and only the exchange rate, or with a price ratio and an exchange rate.

Lastly, estimates of import demand elasticities which produced a "wrong" sign on any of the variables were omitted from the following tables. We viewed a wrong sign on any coefficient as a plausible indication of specification error and/or difficulties with the sample period data. As a result, such empirical estimates were omitted. The omitting of these estimates did not result in the deletion of a large number of studies, but one should be aware of this aspect of the results reported in the tables.

Tables 3.1 through 3.3 provide a total of 658 estimates of the demand for imports, and each of the tables are structured as follows. The first column contains the name(s) of the author(s) followed by the year of publication in parentheses. Below the author(s) name(s), the time period utilized to estimate the parameters is reported. If no numbers appear after the year, the data employed in the analysis was annual data. In the second column, estimates of the income elasticity are presented. For all parameter estimates a * denotes statistical significance at the .05 level of significance or higher. The results of the price-ratio specifications are given in the third column. Columns four, five, and six present the estimated elasticities for import prices (PM), domestic price (PD), and the exchange rate (XR) separately. Thus, it is relatively simple to determine the specification which was employed in the study.

Table 3.1 contains estimates of the demand for aggregate or total merchandise imports and estimates for the demand for imported goods and services together. In total, Table 3.1 presents a total of 337 estimates covering 82 countries. Three broad conclusions stand out. First, the primary specification used in estimating import demand is the price-ratio specification (Equation 3.1). The split-price specification is the second most commonly used specification (Equation 3.2). The specification employing both split prices and the exchange rate is seldom used (Equation 3.3). Second, the estimated income elasticities of demand generally fall in the range of 1 to 2. Third, the estimated price elasticities of demand are generally small and are in the range of 0 to -1.

Since the quantity of imported oil, energy products, agricultural products, crude materials, etc. may be less responsive to changes in income and relative prices, it is common to estimate the elasticities for total imports minus various offending categories. Table 3.2 contains estimates of the demand for total imports minus various sub-categories of imports. In total, Table 3.2 presents a total of 53 estimates covering 19 countries.

Lastly, Table 3.3 presents estimates of the demand for imports for rather broad product categories. In total, Table 3.3 presents at total of 268 estimates covering 33 countries. It is important to note at this point that further degrees and types of disaggregation are available but not include in the following tables.

Estimates are available for very narrowly defined product categories. Studies in the area include Clark (1977), Mutti (1977), Shiells (1985), Shiells, Stern, and Deardorff (1986), Lawrence (1987), Shiells (1991), Feenstra (1994), Wilde et al., (1986), Wu (1992), Lachler (1985). Ajayi (1985), Umo (1991), Athukorala and Menon (1995), Menon (1995) Weisskoff (1979), Haniotis (1990), Biswas and Ram (1980) Sarmad and Mahmood (1985, 1987) Bautista (1980), and Hamilton (1980).

It is also possible to obtain estimates of total country imports by country. Studies analyzing imports of a particular country by country include Phuap (1981), Geraci and Prewo (1982), Dudly (1983), Haynes, Hutchison, and Mikesell (1986), Bergstrand (1987), Cline (1989), Marquez (1990, 1992), Craig (1986), Dudley (1983), Kumar and Akbar (1983), Lawson and Thanassoulas (1982), Caporale and Doroodian (1994), Fullerton, et al. (1997), and Khan (1975).

A final category of import demand elasticities not included in the tables are imports by product and by country/region. Studies in this area include Sazanami and Matsumura (1985), Marquez (1988), Marquez and McNeilly (1988), Parthama and Vincent (1992), Paramosathy and Phillips (1985), Kumar and Akbar (1983), Heien and Pick (1991).

Table 3.1   Import Demand Elasticities by Country
Total Merchandise Imports

COUNTRY		Category			
Author, (Year) Period	Y	PM/PD	PM	PD	XR
ARGENTINA		**Total Imports**			
Agarwal, (1984) 1970-1978	2.06*	-0.408*			2.09
Faini, et al., (1988) 1964-1980	2.56*	-2.1*			
Cline, (1989) 1973:1-1987:4	2.42*	-0.32*			
Clavijo and Faini, (1990) 1967-1987	1.403*	-7.54*			

* denotes statistical significance at the .05 level

Table 3.1 (Continued)

COUNTRY Author, (Year) Period	Y	Category			
		PM/PD	PM	PD	XR
AUSTRALIA		**Goods and Services**			
Andersen, (1993) 1960-1990	1.25	-0.38			
		Total Imports			
Warner and Kreinin, (1983) 1972:1-1980:2	0.15		-0.55*	0.95*	0.87*
Katayama, et al., (1987) 1970:1-1980:4	1.826*	-2.242			
Wilkinson, (1992) 1974:3-1989:3	1.85*	-0.63*			
Bewley and Orden, (1994) 1972:3-1989:3	1.609*	-0.572*			
Bahmani-O. and Niroomand, (1998) 1960-1992	1.10*	-0.57*			
AUSTRIA		**Goods and Services**			
Andersen, (1993) 1960-1990	1.85	-0.33			

* denotes statistical significance at the .05 level

Table 3.1 (Continued)

COUNTRY		Category			
Author, (Year) Period	Y	PM/PD PM		PD	XR

AUSTRIA (Continued)

Total Imports

Akhtar, (1980) 1960-1976	1.820*	-0.383*			
Goldstein, et al., (1980) 1950-1973	1.555*	-0.980*			
Warner and Kreinin, (1983) 1972:1-1980:1	0.54*		-0.10	0.43	0.84
Bahmani-O. and Niroomand, (1998) 1960-1992	1.96*	-0.53*			

BANGLADESH

Total Imports

Nguyen and Bhuyan, (1977) 1954-1968	1.484	-0.385			
Faini, et al., (1988) 1964-1980	1.52*	-0.36*			
Kabir, (1988) 1973:1-1984:4	1.71*	-0.39*			

* denotes statistical significance at the .05 level

Table 3.1 (Continued)

COUNTRY	Category				
Author, (Year) Period	Y	PM/PD	PM	PD	XR

BELGIUM

Goods and Services

Andersen, (1993) 1960-1990	1.82	-0.17			

Total Imports

Goldstein and Khan, (1976) 1955:1-1973:4	1.781*	-0.593*			
Akhtar, (1980) 1960-1976	1.954*	-0.673*			
Boylan, et al., (1980) 1953-1975	1.75*	-0.17			
Goldstein, et al., (1980) 1950-1973	1.983*	-0.510*			
Warner and Kreinin, (1983) 1972:1-1979:4	2.32*		-0.24	0.30	0.56
Welsch, (1987) 1962-1981	0.5927*	-0.6117*			
Urbain, (1992) 1953-1985	1.3707*		-0.5735*	0.7411*	
Bahmani-O. and Niroomand, (1998) 1960-1992	1.82*	-0.80*			

* denotes statistical significance at the .05 level

Table 3.1 (Continued)

COUNTRY		Category			
Author, (Year) Period	Y	PM/PD PM		PD	XR

BELGIUM-LUXEMBOURG

Total Imports

Beenstock and Minford, (1976) 1955:1-1971:4	1.498*	-2.857*			

BENIN

Total Imports

Arize and Afifi, (1987) 1960-1982	2.19*		-0.79*	2.96*	

BOLIVIA

Total Imports

Faini, et al., (1988) 1964-1980	1.11*	-0.44*			

BRAZIL

Total Imports

Lemgruber, (1976) 1965-1974	1.49*	-0.49*			
Weisskoff, (1979) 1953-1970	2.33*	-0.37*			
Agarwal, (1984) 1969-1978	1.670*	-0.762*			-1.86

* denotes statistical significance at the .05 level

Table 3.1 (Continued)

COUNTRY	Category				
Author, (Year) Period	Y	PM/PD	PM	PD	XR
BRAZIL (Continued) **Total Imports**					
Bahmani-Oskooee, (1986) 1974:1-1980:4	0.910*	-0.0691			0.0128*
Faini, et al., (1988) 1964-1980	0.63	-1.1			
Zini, (1988) 1970:1-1986:3	1.28*		-0.181*	0.099	
Cline, (1989) 1973:1-1987:4	0.42*	-0.56			
BURKINA FASO **Total Imports**					
Arize and Afifi, (1987) 1960-1982	1.2*		-0.93*	1.14*	
CAMEROON **Total Imports**					
Arize and Afifi, (1987) 1960-1982	1.49*	-1.05*			

---

* denotes statistical significance at the .05 level

Table 3.1 (Continued)

COUNTRY		Category			
Author, (Year) Period	Y	PM/PD	PM	PD	XR
CANADA					
		Goods and Services			
Andersen, (1993) 1960-1990	1.47	-0.50			
		Total Imports			
Yadav, (1975) 1956:1-1972:4	1.108*	-2.490*			
Beenstock and Minford, (1976) 1955:1-1971:4	0.887*	-1.578*			
Murray and Ginman, (1976) 1950:3-1964:4	0.51*		-0.72*	1.26*	
Khan and Ross, (1977) 1960-1972	1.66*	-0.99			
Yadav, (1977) 1956:1-1973:4	1.259*	-1.371*			
Wilson and Tackas, (1979) 1957-1971	1.868*		-2.751	1.203	-2.750
Akhtar, (1980) 1960-1976	1.657*	-0.609*			
Goldstein, et al., (1980) 1950-1973	1.412*	-0.779*			

* denotes statistical significance at the .05 level

Table 3.1 (Continued)

COUNTRY	Category			
Author, (Year) Period	Y	PM/PD PM	PD	XR

CANADA (Continued)

Total Imports (Continued)

	Y	PM/PD	PM	PD	XR
Warner and Kreinin, (1983) 1972:1-1980:4	0.25		-0.74*	0.97*	0.28
Thursby and Thursby, (1984) 1957:1-1977:4	1.35*	-0.46*			
Welsch, (1987) 1962-1981	0.4155*	-0.4342*			
Cline, (1989) 1973:1-1987:4	2.01*	-2.35*			
Dunlevy and Deyak, (1989) 1957:1-1982:2	1.24*		-0.46*	0.67*	
Asseery and Peel, (1991) 1972:2-1986:4	1.47*	-1.47*			
Deyak, et al., (1993) 1958:1-1989:4	1.6566*		-0.8180*	0.7169*	0.7853*
Marquez, (1996) 1952-1992	1.58*	-0.72*			
Amano and Wirjanto, (1997) 1960:1-1993:3	1.579*	-0.508*			
Bahmani-O. and Niroomand, (1998) 1960-1992	1.31*	-0.67			

* denotes statistical significance at the .05 level

Table 3.1 (Continued)

COUNTRY		Category			
Author, (Year) Period	Y	PM/PD PM		PD	XR

CENTRAL AFRICAN REPUBLIC

Total Imports

Arize and Afifi, (1987) 1960-1982	0.44		-1.06*	0.87*	
Faini, et al., (1988) 1964-1980	0.57*	-1.87*			

CHILE

Total Imports

Faini, et al., (1988) 1964-1980	2.21*	-0.32*			
Meller and Cabezas, (1989) 1974:1-1987:4	0.910*	-0.580*			

COLOMBIA

Total Imports

Agarwal, (1984) 1970-1979	1.53*	-0.986			-2.56
Faini, et al., (1988) 1964-1980	1.25*	-0.52			
Clavijo and Faini, (1990) 1967-1987	1.263*	-0.499*			

* denotes statistical significance at the .05 level

Table 3.1 (Continued)

COUNTRY	Category				
Author, (Year) Period	Y	PM/PD	PM	PD	XR
CONGO		Total Imports			
Arize and Afifi, (1987) 1960-1982	0.77*			-0.63*	2.13*
COTE D' IVOIRE		Total Imports			
Arize, (1987) 1960-1982	0.39			-0.78*	0.70
Arize and Afifi, (1987) 1960-1982	1.26*			-0.78*	0.70*
Faini, et al., (1992) 1961-1985	1.6*	-1.58*			
CYPRUS		Total Imports			
Asseery and Perdikis, (1991) 1960-1987	1.45*			-0.32*	0.31*
DENMARK		Goods and Services			
Andersen, (1993) 1960-1990	1.48	-0.14			

* denotes statistical significance at the .05 level

Table 3.1 (Continued)

COUNTRY	Category				
Author, (Year) Period	Y	PM/PD	PM	PD	XR

DENMARK (Continued)

Total Imports

Goldstein and Khan, (1976) 1955:3-1973:4	1.049*	-0.760*			
Akhtar, (1980) 1960-1976	1.524*	-0.686*			
Boylan, et al., (1980) 1953-1975	1.58*	-0.52*			
Goldstein, et al., (1980) 1950-1973	1.417*	-0.754*			
Warner and Kreinin, (1983) 1972:1-1979:4	1.02*		-0.47	0.73	-0.28
Bahmani-O. and Niroomand, (1998) 1960-1992	1.17	-0.81			

ECUADOR

Total Imports

Agarwal, (1984) 1970-1978	1.89*	-0.308			-3.98

* denotes statistical significance at the .05 level

Table 3.1 (Continued)

COUNTRY	Category				
Author, (Year) Period	Y	PM/PD	PM	PD	XR

ETHIOPIA

Total Imports

Umo, (1981) 1963-1977	1.61*	-3.05*			
Tegene, (1989) 1973:1-1985:4	0.19	-0.88*			0.28*

FINLAND

Goods and Services

Andersen, (1993) 1960-1990	1.35	-0.05			

Total Imports

Goldstein and Khan, (1976) 1955:3-1973:4	1.580*	-0.337*			
Goldstein, et al., (1980) 1950-1973	1.651*	-0.277			
Agarwal, (1984) 1970-1979	2.25*	-0.998*			3.08
Aurikko, (1985) 1963:1-1983:4	1.50*	-0.74*			
Aurikko, (1985) 1964:1-1983:4	1.23*	-0.52*			

* denotes statistical significance at the .05 level

Table 3.1 (Continued)

COUNTRY		Category			
Author, (Year) Period	Y	PM/PD PM		PD	XR
FRANCE		**Goods and Services**			
Andersen, (1993) 1960-1990	1.83	-0.22			
		Total Imports			
Beenstock and Minford, (1976) 1955:1-1971:4	1.589*	-1.3*			
Akhtar, (1979) 1969:1-1978:4	2.3*	-0.5*			
Wilson and Tackas, (1979) 1957-1971	1.070*		-1.218	1.761	-1.216
Akhtar, (1980) 1960-1976	1.895*	-0.484*			
Warner and Kreinin, (1983) 1972:1-1980:3	0.30		-0.36	1.20*	1.48*
Welsch, (1987) 1962-1981	0.5267*	-0.5717*			
Cline, (1989) 1973:1-1987:4	2.68*	-0.57*			
Bahmani-O. and Niroomand, (1998) 1960-1992	1.52	-0.42*			

* denotes statistical significance at the .05 level

Table 3.1 (Continued)

COUNTRY	Category				
Author, (Year) Period	Y	PM/PD	PM	PD	XR
GABON					
		Total Imports			
Arize and Afifi, (1987) 1960-1982	0.87*	-0.90*			
Faini, et al., (1988) 1964-1980	1.53*	-1.33*			
GAMBIA					
		Total Imports			
Arize and Afifi, (1987) 1960-1982	1.45*			-1.38*	1.26*
Clavijo and Faini, (1990) 1967-1987	1.283*	-1.034*			
GERMANY					
		Goods and Services			
Andersen, (1993) 1960-1990	2.02	-0.06			
		Total Imports			
Beenstock and Minford, (1976) 1955:1-1971:4	1.059*	-0.417*			

* denotes statistical significance at the .05 level

Table 3.1 (Continued)

COUNTRY	Category				
Author, (Year) Period	Y	PM/PD	PM	PD	XR
GERMANY (Continued)					
	Total Imports (Continued)				
Goldstein and Khan, (1976) 1955:1-1973:4	2.089*	-0.598*			
Akhtar, (1979) 1969:1-1978:4	3.2*	-0.4*			
Wilson and Tackas, (1979) 1957-1971	1.460*		-0.118	1.91	0.116
Akhtar, (1980) 1960-1976	2.046*	-0.510*			
Goldstein, et al., (1980) 1950-1973	1.671*	-0.469*			
Phaup, (1981) 1958-1978	2.14*		-0.63*	0.39	
Warner and Kreinin, (1983) 1972:1-1980:3	2.09*		-0.50*	0.83*	0.41*
Thursby and Thursby, (1984) 1960:1-1978:2	1.59*	-0.30*			
Katayama, et al., (1987) 1970:1-1980:4	1.220*	-0.449*			
Welsch, (1987) 1962-1981	0.2801*	-0.2844*			

* denotes statistical significance at the .05 level

Table 3.1 (Continued)

COUNTRY		Category			
Author, (Year) Period	Y	PM/PD	PM	PD	XR

GERMANY (Continued)

Total Imports (Continued)

Cline, (1989) 1973:1-1987:4	2.26	-0.48*			
Asseery and Peel, (1991) 1972:2-1986:4	1.97*	-0.33*			
Bahmani-O. and Niroomand, (1998) 1960-1992	1.98*	-0.55*			

GREECE

Total Imports

Petoussis, (1981) 1960-1979	1.000		-0.409*	0.534*	
Bahmani-Oskooee, (1986) 1973:1-1980:4	0.927*	-0.4216			0.0039
Sarmad, (1988) 1960-1981	0.646*	-0.711*			
Clavijo and Faini, (1990) 1967-1987	1.404*	-0.028			
Bahmani-O. and Niroomand, (1998) 1960-1992	1.74*	-0.48*			

* denotes statistical significance at the .05 level

Table 3.1 (Continued)

COUNTRY	Category				
Author, (Year) Period	Y	PM/PD	PM	PD	XR
GUYANA Total Imports					
Gafar, (1995) 1961-1990	1.29*	-0.32*			
INDIA Total Imports					
Nguyen and Bhuyan, (1977) 1957-1969	1.762*	-0.728			
Bahmani-Oskooee, (1986) 1973:1-1979:3	0.088	-0.4964*			0.0064
Sundararajan and Bhole, (1989) 1960-1983	0.4407*	-0.1228*			
Clark, (1992) 1971:4-1986:3	0.55*		-0.34*	0.92*	
INDONESIA Total Imports					
Faini, et al., (1988) 1964-1980	1.02	-1.5			
Clavijo and Faini, (1990) 1967-1987	1.067*	-0.325			

* denotes statistical significance at the .05 level

Table 3.1 (Continued)

COUNTRY	Category				
Author, (Year) Period	Y	PM/PD	PM	PD	XR
IRAN		Total Imports			
Clark, (1992) 1971:4-1986:3	1.67*		-1.29*	0.47*	
IRELAND		Total Imports			
Boylan, et al., (1979) 1953-1975	1.56*	-0.68*			
Boylan, et al., (1980) 1953-1975	1.84*	-0.45*			
Boylan, et al., (1981) 1953-1975	1.88*	-0.30			
Warner and Kreinin, (1983) 1972:1-1979:4	0.10*		-0.67*	0.89*	0.11
Boylan and Cuddy, (1987) 1953-1976	1.565*	-1.400*			
ISRAEL		Total Imports			
Bahmani-Oskooee, (1986) 1973:1-1980:4	0.0313	-0.00015			-0.0159

* denotes statistical significance at the .05 level

Table 3.1 (Continued)

COUNTRY		Category			
Author, (Year) Period	Y	PM/PD PM		PD	XR

ISRAEL (Continued)

Total Imports (Continued)

Arize and Afifi, (1987) 1960-1982	1.64*	-1.18*			
Faini, et al., (1988) 1964-1980	1.43*	-0.66*			
Clavijo and Faini, (1990) 1967-1987	0.944	-0.195			

ITALY

Goods and Services

Andersen, (1993) 1960-1990	1.62	-0.22			

Total Imports

Akhtar, (1980) 1960-1976	1.906*	-0.511*			
Goldstein, et al., (1980) 1950-1973	2.092*	-0.138			
Mastropasqua, (1982) 1960:1-1979:4	1.0702*	-0.1560			
Gandolfo and Petit, (1983) 1960:1-1980:4	1.8614*	-0.1136			

* denotes statistical significance at the .05 level

Table 3.1 (Continued)

COUNTRY	Category				
Author, (Year) **Period**	Y	PM/PD	PM	PD	XR

ITALY (Continued)

Total Imports (Continued)

Warner and Kreinin, (1983) 1972:1-1979:1	3.10*		-0.75*	1.11*	1.53*
Welsch, (1987) 1962-1981	0.3350*	-0.3242*			
Cline, (1989) 1973:1-1987:4	2.48*	-0.49*			
Giovennetti, (1989) 1970:1-1986:2	0.83*	-0.235*			
Bahmani-O. and Niroomand, (1998) 1960-1992	1.73*	-0.43*			

JAPAN

Goods and Services

Andersen, (1993) 1960-1990	1.25	-0.21			

Total Imports

Beenstock and Minford, (1976) 1955:1-1971:4	1.649*	-1.29*			
Khan and Ross, (1977) 1960-1972	0.13*	-0.64*			

* denotes statistical significance at the .05 level

Table 3.1 (Continued)

COUNTRY	Category				
Author, (Year) Period	Y	PM/PD	PM	PD	XR
JAPAN (Continued)		**Total Imports** (Continued)			
Wilson and Tackas, (1979) 1957:1-1971:4	1.686*		-1.251	7.693	-1.254
Akhtar, (1980) 1960-1976	1.281*	-0.177			
Warner and Kreinin, (1983) 1972:1-1980:3	0.89		-0.08	0.05	0.25
Thursby and Thursby, (1984) 1957:4-1977:4	1.17*	-0.33*			
Lawrence, (1987) 1970-1985	0.80*				1.07*
Loopesko and Johnson, (1988) 1968:1-1986:4	1.07*	-0.44*			
Cline, (1989) 1973:1-1987:4	1.21*	-0.69*			
Noland, (1989) 1970:1-1985:4	1.66*	-0.67*			
Ohtani, et al., (1990) 1975:1-1986:4	0.737*	-0.253*			
Asseery and Peel, (1991) 1972:2-1986:4	1.36*	-0.64*			

* denotes statistical significance at the .05 level

Table 3.1 (Continued)

COUNTRY	Category				
Author, (Year) Period	Y	PM/PD	PM	PD	XR
JAPAN (Continued)		**Total Imports** (Continued)			
Arize and Walker, (1992) 1973:1-1988:4	1.31*		-0.348*	0.85*	0.693*
Deyak, et al., (1993) 1958:1-1985:4	1.1076*		-1.0351*	0.8897*	0.7038*
Urbain, (1996) 1966:1-1994:1	1.00*	-0.589*			
Marquez, (1996) 1952-1992	1.09*	-0.66*			
Ceglowski, (1997) 1976:1-1993:4	0.94*	-0.46*			
Bahmani-O. and Niroomand, (1998) 1960-1992	0.46*	-0.97*			
JAMAICA		**Total Imports**			
Gafar, (1981) 1954-1972	1.12*	-0.58*			
Gafar, (1984) 1954-1972	0.39*	-0.05			

* denotes statistical significance at the .05 level

Table 3.1 (Continued)

COUNTRY		Category			
Author, (Year) Period	Y	PM/PD PM	PD	XR

JAMAICA (Continued)

Total Imports (Continued)

Faini, et al., (1988) 1964-1980	1.12*	-0.18			
Clavijo and Faini, (1990) 1967-1987	1.232*	-0.314*			
Gafar, (1995) 1961-1986	1.44*	-0.26*			

KENYA

Total Imports

Faini, et al., (1988) 1964-1980	1.37*	-1.48*			
Sarmad, (1988) 1960-1981	0.885*	-0.848*			
Tegene, (1989) 1973:1-1985:4	2.03*	-2.12*			0.13*

KOREA

Total Imports

Agarwal, (1984) 1970-1978	2.89*	-0.890*			2.36

* denotes statistical significance at the .05 level

Table 3.1 (Continued)

COUNTRY	Category				
Author, (Year) Period	Y	PM/PD	PM	PD	XR
KOREA (Continued)					
	Total Imports (Continued)				
Bahmani-Oskooee, (1984) 1975:1-1979:4	1.706*	-0.373*			
Bahmani-Oskooee, (1986) 1973:1-1980:4	1.394*	-0.432*			
Katayama, et al., (1987) 1970:1-1980:4	0.121	-1.353*			
Faini, et al., (1988) 1964-1980	1.50*	-0.22			
Moreno, (1989) 1974:1-1989:4	1.08*	-0.74*			
Clavijo and Faini, (1990) 1967-1987	1.291*	-0.405*			
Arize and Spalding, (1991) 1973:1-1985:4	0.1600*			-0.5069*	0.6773*
Mah, (1993) 1981:1-1988:4	1.246*	-3.046*			
Bahmani-Oskooee and Rhee, (1997) 1971:1-1988:4	1.21	-0.11			
Bahmani-O. and Niroomand, (1998) 1960-1992	1.83*	-0.13			

* denotes statistical significance at the .05 level

Table 3.1 (Continued)

COUNTRY		Category			
Author, (Year) Period	Y	PM/PD PM		PD	XR
KUWAIT		**Total Imports**			
Asseery and Perdikis, (1990) 1970-1985	1.287*	-0.721*			
Asseery and Perdikis, (1993) 1963-1985	1.551*	-0.784*			
LIBERIA		**Total Imports**			
Arize and Afifi, (1987) 1960-1982	0.96*	-0.57*			
LIBYA		**Total Imports**			
Clavijo and Faini, (1990) 1967-1987	1.004*	-1.194*			
Faini, et al., (1992) 1961-1985	0.64*	-1.21*			
MALAWI		**Total Imports**			
Arize, (1987) 1960-1982	0.32	-0.51*			

* denotes statistical significance at the .05 level

Table 3.1 (Continued)

COUNTRY	Category				
Author, (Year) Period	Y	PM/PD	PM	PD	XR
MALAWI (Continued)		**Total Imports** (Continued)			
Arize and Afifi, (1987) 1960-1982	0.32	-0.51*			
MALAYSIA		**Total Imports**			
Faini, et al., (1988) 1964-1980	1.67*	-2.3			
Arize, (1991) 1973:1-1986:4	2.2*		-0.08	1.08*	
MALI		**Total Imports**			
Arize and Afifi, (1987) 1960-1982	0.06		-0.63*	1.18*	
MAURITIUS		**Total Imports**			
Arize, (1987) 1960-1982	1.2*		-1.07*	1.12*	
Tegene, (1989) 1973:1-1985:4	0.93*	-1.39*			0.37*

* denotes statistical significance at the .05 level

Table 3.1 (Continued)

COUNTRY		Category			
Author, (Year) Period	Y	PM/PD PM	PD	XR

MAURITIUS (Continued)

Total Imports (Continued)

Bahmani-O. and Niroomand, (1998) 1960-1992	1.05*	-0.93*			

MEXICO

Total Imports

Agarwal, (1984) 1970-1979	3.86*	-0.563			8.34
Cline, (1989) 1973:1-1987:4	1.69*	-0.51*			
Clavijo and Faini, (1990) 1967-1987	1.213*	-1.044*			
Faini, et al., (1992) 1961-1985	1.29*	-1.12*			

MOROCCO

Total Imports

Arize and Afifi, (1987) 1960-1982	1.93*		-0.67*	1.4*	
Faini, et al,, (1988) 1964-1980	1.38*	-0.42			

---

* denotes statistical significance at the .05 level

Table 3.1 (Continued)

COUNTRY		Category			
Author, (Year) Period	Y	PM/PD PM		PD	XR
MOROCCO (Continued)		**Total Imports** (Continued)			
Sarmad, (1988) 1960-1981	1.737	-0.072			
NETHERLANDS		**Goods and Services**			
Andersen, (1993) 1960-1990	1.86	-0.15			
		Total Imports			
Akhtar, (1980) 1960-1976	1.667*	-0.197*			
Warner and Kreinin, (1983) 1972:1-1979:4	2.17*		-0.29*	0.11	0.58*
Welsch, (1987) 1962-1981	0.4825*	-0.4638*			
Urbain, (1992) 1952-1985	1.2366*		-0.2393*	0.7595*	
Bahmani-O. and Niroomand, (1998) 1960-1992	1.24*	-0.96*			

* denotes statistical significance at the .05 level

Table 3.1 (Continued)

COUNTRY	Category				
Author, (Year) Period	Y	PM/PD	PM	PD	XR
NEW ZEALAND		**Total Imports**			
Warner and Kreinin, (1983) 1972:1-1979:4	2.68*		-0.64*	0.97*	1.69
NIGER		**Total Imports**			
Arize and Afifi, (1987) 1960-1982	1.18*		-1.40*	2.07*	
NIGERIA		**Total Imports**			
Ajayi, (1985) 1960-1970	0.257*	-2.718*			
Arize, (1987) 1960-1974	1.07*	-0.36			
Salehi-Isfahini, (1989) 1963-1979	0.69*	-1.15*			
Umo, (1991) 1960-1985	0.722*	-0.175*			
Nyatepe-Coo and Akorlie, (1994) 1960-1990	0.1344*				-0.2500*

* denotes statistical significance at the .05 level

Table 3.1 (Continued)

COUNTRY	Category			
Author, (Year) Period	Y	PM/PD PM	PD	XR
NORWAY		**Total Imports**		
Goldstein and Khan, (1976) 1955:3-1973:4	0.984*	-0.858*		
Akhtar, (1980) 1960-1976	1.562*	-0.663*		
Warner and Kreinin, (1983) 1971:3-1978:4	0.68*	-0.76*	0.51*	2.56
OMAN		**Total Imports**		
Asseery and Perdikis, (1991) 1970-1985	1.175*	-0.264		
Asseery and Perdikis, (1993) 1963-1985	1.221*	-0.02		
PAKISTAN		**Total Imports**		
Nguyen and Bhuyan, (1977) 1954-1968	2.381*	-1.352*		
Arize and Afifi, (1987) 1960-1982	0.42	-1.12*	2.30*	

* denotes statistical significance at the .05 level

Table 3.1 (Continued)

COUNTRY		Category			
Author, (Year) Period	Y	PM/PD	PM	PD	XR

PAKISTAN (Continued)

Total Imports (Continued)

Sarmad and Mahmood, (1987) 1969-1984	1.290*	-0.230*			
Faini, et al., (1988) 1964-1980	0.76*	-0.48*			
Sarmad, (1989) 1959-1986	0.631*	-0.669*			
Clavijo and Faini, (1990) 1967-1987	0.997*	-0.556*			
Shabbir and Mahmood, (1991) 1959-1988	1.20*	-0.72*			

PARAGUAY

Total Imports

Faini, et al., (1988) 1964-1980	1.42*	-0.56			
Clavijo and Faini, (1990) 1967-1987	0.672*	-0.478			

---

* denotes statistical significance at the .05 level

Table 3.1 (Continued)

COUNTRY	Category			
Author, (Year) **Period**	Y	PM/PD PM	PD	XR
PERU		Total Imports		
Agarwal, (1984) 1970-1979	1.02*	-0.486*		7.56
Faini, et al., (1988) 1964-1980	1.66*	-0.40*		
Sarmad, (1988) 1960-1981	0.472	-0.679*		
Clavijo and Faini, (1990) 1967-1987	0.522*	-0.646*		
PHILIPPINES		Total Imports		
Agarwal, (1984) 1970-1978	3.08*	-0.987*		-3.56*
Faini, et al., (1988) 1964-1980	1.2*	-0.56*		
Clavijo and Faini, (1990) 1967-1987	1.012*	-0.250		
Arize, (1991) 1973:1-1985:4	0.69*	-1.36*		

* denotes statistical significance at the .05 level

Table 3.1 (Continued)

COUNTRY		Category			
Author, (Year) Period	Y	PM/PD PM		PD	XR

PHILIPPINES (Continued)

Total Imports (Continued)

Bahmani-O. and Niroomand, (1998) 1960-1992	1.35*	-1.01*			

PORTUGAL

Total Imports

Sarmad, (1988) 1960-1981	0.970*	-0.927*			
Faini, et al., (1992) 1961-1985	2.24*	-1.58*			

QATAR

Total Imports

Asseery and Perdikis, (1990) 1970-1985	0.867*	-1.206*			
Asseery and Perdikis, (1993) 1970-1985	0.407*	-0.896*			

SAUDI ARABIA

Total Imports

Asseery and Perdikis, (1990) 1970-1985	1.142*	-3.497*			

* denotes statistical significance at the .05 level

Table 3.1 (Continued)

COUNTRY	Category				
Author, (Year) Period	Y	PM/PD	PM	PD	XR
SAUDI ARABIA (Continued)					
Total Imports (Continued)					
Clark, (1992) 1971:4-1986:3	2.139*			-0.539	1.40*
Asseery and Perdikis, (1993) 1963-1985	0.340*	-1.221*			
Doroodian, et al., (1994) 1963-1990	0.2174*			-0.6763*	1.3334*
SENEGAL					
Total Imports					
Clavijo and Faini, (1990) 1967-1987	1.307*	-0.282			
Faini, et al., (1992) 1961-1985	2.43*	-0.35			
SIERRA LEONE					
Total Imports					
Arize and Afifi, (1987) 1960-1982	1.29*			-0.47*	0.48*

* denotes statistical significance at the .05 level

Table 3.1 (Continued)

COUNTRY		Category			
Author, (Year) Period	Y	PM/PD PM	PD	XR	

SOMALIA

Total Imports

Arize and Afifi, (1987) 1960-1982	1.15*		-0.26	0.72*	

SOUTH AFRICA

Total Imports

Erasmus, (1978) 1965:1-1976:4	0.886*	-1.525*			
Bahmani-Oskooee, (1984) 1975:4-1978:4	1.889	-0.467			
Bahmani-Oskooee, (1986) 1973:1-1980:4	2.499*	-2.46*		-0.1092*	
Bahmani-O. and Niroomand, (1998) 1960-1992	1.29	-0.83			

SPAIN

Goods and Services

Andersen, (1993) 1960-1990	1.89	-0.23			

* denotes statistical significance at the .05 level

Table 3.1 (Continued)

COUNTRY		Category			
Author, (Year) Period	Y	PM/PD	PM	PD	XR

SPAIN (Continued)

Total Imports

Warner and Kreinin, (1983) 1972:1-1979:4	0.75		-0.47*	0.82*	1.27*
Bahmani-O. and Niroomand, (1998) 1960-1992	1.64*	-0.77*			

SWEDEN

Goods and Services

Andersen, (1993) 1960-1990	1.75	-0.10			

Total Imports

Goldstein and Khan, (1976) 1955:3-1973:4	1.332*	-0.397*			
Goldstein, et al., (1980) 1950-1973	1.886*	-0.118			
Bahmani-O. and Niroomand, (1998) 1960-1992	1.69*	-0.19*			

* denotes statistical significance at the .05 level

Table 3.1 (Continued)

COUNTRY			Category		
Author, (Year) Period	**Y**	**PM/PD**	**PM**	**PD**	**XR**
SWITZERLAND					
		Goods and Services			
Andersen, (1993) 1960-1990	1.37	-0.95			
		Total Imports			
Akhtar, (1980) 1960-1976	1.980*	-0.590			
SYRIA					
		Total Imports			
Agarwal, (1984) 1969-1978	1.76*	-0.102*			-0.782
TAIWAN					
		Total Imports			
Agarwal, (1984) 1970-1979	2.89*	-0.203*			0.986*
Cline, (1989) 1973:1-1987:4	1.31*	-0.42*			
Moreno, (1989) 1974:1-1987:4	0.82*	-1.44*			

* denotes statistical significance at the .05 level

Table 3.1 (Continued)

COUNTRY	Category				
Author, (Year) Period	Y	PM/PD	PM	PD	XR
THAILAND		Total Imports			
Bahmani-Oskooee, (1986) 1973:1-1980:4	0.933*	-0.356*			-0.339*
Faini, et al., (1988) 1964-1980	1.25*	-0.67*			
Arize, (1991) 1973:1-1986:4	0.56*		-0.558	0.998*	
Koshal, et al., (1993) 1961-1985	1.02*	-1.00*			
TOGO		Total Imports			
Arize and Afifi, (1987) 1960-1982	1.58*	-2.2*			
TRINIDAD and TOBAGO		Total Imports			
Gafar, (1995) 1967-1990	2.29*	-0.34			

* denotes statistical significance at the .05 level

Table 3.1 (Continued)

COUNTRY		Category			
Author, (Year) Period	Y	PM/PD PM		PD	XR
TUNISIA		**Total Imports**			
Arize, (1987) 1960-1982	0.46*	-0.35			
Arize and Afifi, (1987) 1960-1982	0.46*	-0.35			
Faini, et al., (1988) 1964-1980	1.43*	-0.25			
Tegene, (1989) 1973:1-1985:4	2.61*	-0.13*			0.33*
Bahmani-O. and Niroomand, (1998) 1960-1992	1.52*	-0.63*			
TURKEY		**Total Imports**			
Tansel and Togan, (1987) 1960-1985	0.6765*	-0.305*			
UGANDA		**Total Imports**			
Arize and Afifi, (1987) 1960-1982	1.7*		-1.3*	2.04*	

* denotes statistical significance at the .05 level

Table 3.1 (Continued)

COUNTRY	Category				
Author, (Year) Period	Y	PM/PD	PM	PD	XR

UNITED ARAB EMIRATES

Total Imports

Asseery and Pedikis, (1990) 1970-1985	0.888*	-0.480			
Asseery and Pedikis, (1993) 1970-1985	1.023*	-0.466			

UNITED KINGDOM

Total Imports

Akhtar, (1979) 1968:1-1978:3	3.9*	-2.9*			
Akhtar, (1980) 1960-1976	2.120*	-0.139*			
Phaup, (1981) 1958-1978	3.22*			-0.22*	0.04*
Beenstock and Warburton, (1982) 1950-1979	0.9124*	-0.2279*			
Petoussis, (1985) 1960:1-1979:4	0.986*			-0.537*	1.441*
Welsch, (1987) 1962-1981	0.3249*	-0.3242*			

---

* denotes statistical significance at the .05 level

Table 3.1 (Continued)

COUNTRY		Category			
Author, (Year) Period	Y	PM/PD PM		PD	XR

UNITED KINGDOM (Continued)

Total Imports (Continued)

Cline, (1989) 1973:1-1987:4	2.35	-1.04*			
Asseery and Peel, (1991) 1972:2-1986:4	2.37*	-0.07			
Bahmani-O. and Niroomand, (1998) 1.76* 1960-1992		-0.28*			

UNITED STATES

Goods and Services

Andersen, (1993) 1960-1990	2.00	-0.17			

Total Imports

Beenstock and Minford, (1976) 1955:1-1971:4	0.943*	-1.042*			
Goldstein and Khan, (1976) 1955:3-1973:4	1.844*	-0.475*			
Murray and Ginman, (1976) 1961:1-1968:4	1.43*		-0.71	3.11*	
Khan and Ross, (1977) 1960:1-1972:4	1.08*	-1.64*			

* denotes statistical significance at the .05 level

Table 3.1 (Continued)

COUNTRY	Category				
Author, (Year) Period	Y	PM/PD	PM	PD	XR

UNITED STATES (Continued)

Total Imports (Continued)

Stern, et al., (1979) 1956:3-1976:2	1.118*		-2.176*	4.122*	
Wilson and Tackas, (1979) 1957:1-1971:4	4.028*		-4.781	8.769	-4.781
Akhtar, (1980) 1960-1976	2.552*	-0.172			
Phaup, (1981) 1958-1978	2.92*		-2.09*	2.53*	
Haynes and Stone, (1982) 1955-1969	1.92*	-0.48			
Volker, (1982) 1958:3-1976:2	1.126*		-0.582*	1.653*	
Haynes and Stone, (1983) 1955:1-1979:4	1.83*		-0.63	1.09	
Haynes and Stone, (1984) 1955-1969	2.25*		-2.83*	1.08*	
Thursby and Thursby, (1984) 1955:1-1978:1	1.72*	-0.20*			
Katayama, et al, (1987). 1970:1-1980:4	2.148*	-1.426			

* denotes statistical significance at the .05 level

Table 3.1 (Continued)

COUNTRY	Category				
Author, (Year) Period	Y	PM/PD	PM	PD	XR

UNITED STATES (Continued)

Total Imports (Continued)

	Y	PM/PD	PM	PD	XR
Welsch, (1987) 1962-1981	0.1322*	-0.1348*			
Di Liberto, (1988) 1962:1-1980:4	3.19*	-3.01*			
Cline, (1989) 1973:1-1987:4	2.44*	-1.36			
Deyak, et al., (1989) 1958:4-1983:4	2.14*	-0.29*			
Moffett, (1989) 1967:1-1987:4	2.48*		-0.68*	0.72*	
Deyak, et al., (1990) 1958:1-1985:4	2.1426*		-0.5363*	0.6599	
Asseery and Peel, (1991) 1972:2-1986:4	2.32*	-0.69*			
Bahmani-Oskooee, (1991) 1973:1-1988:4	2.2030*				-0.0243
Hooper and Marquez, (1993) 1976:3-1992:2	2.50*	-1.03*			
Carone, (1996) 1970:1-1992:4	2.48*		-0.392*	0.398*	

* denotes statistical significance at the .05 level

Table 3.1 (Continued)

COUNTRY	Category				
Author, (Year) Period	Y	PM/PD	PM	PD	XR

UNITED STATES (Continued)

Total Imports (Continued)

Deyak, et al., (1997) 1958:1-1989:2	2.066*			-0.326	0.434
Deyak, et al., (1997) 1958:1-1989:2	2.162*	-0.180			
Deyak, et al., (1997) 1958:1-1971:3	1.335*			-1.319*	3.595*
Deyak, et al., (1997) 1958:1-1971:3	2.017*	-1.401			
Deyak, et al., (1997) 1971:4-1989:2	2.401*			-0.194	0.026
Deyak, et al., (1997) 1971:4-1989:2	2.124*	-0.373*			
Amano and Wirjanto, (1997) 1960:1-1993:3	2.208*	-0.215*			
Bahmani-O. and Niroomand, (1998) 1960-1992	2.07*	-0.34*			

* denotes statistical significance at the .05 level

Table 3.1 (Continued)

COUNTRY Author, (Year) Period	Y	Category			
		PM/PD PM		PD	XR
URUGUAY		**Total Imports**			
Faini, et al., (1988) 1964-1980	2.12*	-0.35*			
Clavijo and Faini, (1990) 1967-1987	1.864*	-0.368*			
VENEZUELA		**Total Imports**			
Khan, (1975) 1953-1972	0.239	-0.897*			
Agarwal, (1984) 1970-1978	1.25*	-0.998*			1.34
Melo and Vogt, (1984) 1962-1979	1.879*	-2.086*			
Sarmad, (1988) 1960-1981	0.078	-1.019*			
WEST AFRICAN MONETARY UNION		**Total Imports**			
Medhora, (1990) 1976-1982	1.42*	-1.06*			

* denotes statistical significance at the .05 level

Table 3.1 (Continued)

COUNTRY	Category				
Author, (Year) Period	Y	PM/PD	PM	PD	XR
ZAMBIA		Total Imports			
Arize, (1987) 1960-1982	0.58*		-0.64*	0.36	
Arize and Afifi, (1987) 1960-1982	0.58*		-0.64*	0.36	
Faini, et al., (1988) 1964-1980	0.78*	-1.14*			
Tegene, (1989) 1973:1-1985:4	0.17	-0.87*			0.046*

* denotes statistical significance at the .05 level

**Table 3.2   Import Demand Elasticities by Country
               Total Merchandise Imports Minus
               Various Categories**

COUNTRY			Category		
Author, (Year) Period	**Y**	**PM/PD**	**PM**	**PD**	**XR**

AUSTRALIA

Non-Oil

Warner and Kreinin, (1983) 1972:1-1980:2	0.20		-0.54*	0.89*	0.75*

Non-Energy

Bosworth, (1993) 1970-1990	1.85*	-0.43*			

AUSTRIA

Non-Oil

Warner and Kreinin, (1983) 1972:1-1980:1	0.64*		-0.72*	0.19	1.47*

Non-Energy

Bosworth, (1993) 1970-1990	1.37*	-0.89*			

BELGIUM

Non-Oil

Warner and Kreinin, (1983) 1972:1-1979:4	1.79*		-0.59*	0.73*	1.04*

* denotes statistical significance at the .05 level

Table 3.2 (Continued)

COUNTRY		Category			
Author, (Year) Period	Y	PM/PD PM		PD	XR

BELGIUM (Continued)

Non-Energy

| Bosworth, (1993) 1970-1990 | 1.23* | -0.99* | | | |

CANADA

Non-Motor Vehicles and Parts

| Yadav, (1975) 1956:1-1972:4 | 0.944* | -1.732* | | | |

Non-Oil

| Akhtar, (1981) 1969:1-1978:1 | 1.47* | -0.69* | | | |
| Warner and Kreinin, (1983) 1972:1-1980:4 | 092* | | -0.55* | 0.68* | 0.20 |

Non-Oil, Non-Motor Vehicles and Parts

| Yadav, (1977) 1956:1-1973:4 | 1.007* | -1.151* | | | |

Non-Energy

| Bosworth, (1993) 1970-1990 | 1.07* | -0.60 | | | |

---

* denotes statistical significance at the .05 level

Table 3.2 (Continued)

COUNTRY	Category				
Author, (Year) Period	Y	PM/PD	PM	PD	XR
DENMARK					
		Non-Oil			
Warner and Kreinin, (1983) 1972:1-1979:4	0.91*		-0.64*	0.64	0.29
		Non-Energy			
Bosworth, (1993) 1970-1990	1.15*	-0.32*			
FINLAND					
		Non-Oil			
Warner and Kreinin, (1983) 1972:1-1979:4	1.31*		-0.69*	0.82*	1.79*
FRANCE					
		Non-Oil			
Akhtar, (1981) 1971:1-1978:1	2.04*	-0.18			
GERMANY					
		Non-Oil			
Akhtar, (1981) 1971:1-1978:1	1.86*	-0.81*			

* denotes statistical significance at the .05 level

Table 3.2 (Continued)

COUNTRY	Category			
Author, (Year) Period	Y	PM/PD PM	PD	XR
GERMANY (Continued)		**Non-Oil** (Continued)		
Warner and Kreinin, (1983) 1971:3-1978:4	2.23*	-1.59*	1.67*	1.45*
		Non-Energy		
Bosworth, (1993) 1970-1990	0.90*	-1.41*		
IRELAND		**Non-Oil**		
Warner and Kreinin, (1983) 1972:1-1979:4	0.10*	-0.31	0.40	0.24
ITALY		**Non-Oil**		
Warner and Kreinin, (1983) 1972:1-1979:1	1.95*	-0.02	0.22	0.38
		Non-Energy		
Bosworth, (1993) 1970-1990	1.94*	-1.77*		

* denotes statistical significance at the .05 level

Table 3.2 (Continued)

COUNTRY	Category				
Author, (Year) Period	Y	PM/PD	PM	PD	XR
JAPAN					
Non-Oil					
Akhtar, (1981) 1968:1-1978:1	1.63*	-0.53*			
Warner and Kreinin, (1983) 1971:3-1978:4	0.55*		-0.46*	0.76*	0.52
Hooper and Marquez, (1993) 1976:4-1992:2	1.03*	-0.73*			
Non-Energy					
Bosworth, (1991) 1970-1990	1.33*	-1.38*			
NETHERLANDS					
Non-Oil					
Warner and Kreinin, (1983) 1971:3-1978:4	3.39*		-0.72*	0.67*	1.14*
Non-Energy					
Bosworth, (1993) 1970-1990	1.23*	-0.61*			

* denotes statistical significance at the .05 level

Table 3.2 (Continued)

COUNTRY	Category				
Author, (Year) Period	Y	PM/PD	PM	PD	XR
NEW ZEALAND		Non-Oil			
Warner and Kreinin, (1983) 1972:1-1979:4	2.11*		-0.29	0.74*	2.07*
PAKISTAN		Non-Oil			
Sarmad and Mahmood, (1987) 1969-1984	1.630*	-0.540*			
SPAIN		Non-Oil			
Warner and Kreinin, (1983) 1972:1-1979:4	0.67		-0.36*	0.62*	1.15*
		Non-Energy			
Buisan and Gordo, (1994) 1964-1992	1.48*	-0.81*			
SWEDEN		Non-Oil			
Warner and Kreinin, (1983) 1971:3-1978:3	3.39		-0.72*	0.67*	1.14*

* denotes statistical significance at the .05 level

Table 3.2 (Continued)

COUNTRY	Category				
Author, (Year) Period	Y	PM/PD	PM	PD	XR

TRINIDAD and TOBAGO

Non-Oil

Gafar, (1988) 1967-1984	3.0050*	-0.5316			

UNITED KINGDOM

Non-Oil

Akhtar, (1981) 1968:1-1978:1	2.66*	-0.93*			
Warner and Kreinin, (1983) 1972:1-1980:3	0.37		-0.15*	1.60*	0.29

UNITED STATES

Non-Oil

Akhtar, (1981) 1967:1-1978:2	2.76*	-1.79*			
Warner and Kreinin, (1983) 1972:1-1980:4	1.37*		-1.19*	1.33*	1.14
Helkie and Hooper, (1987) 1969:1-1984:4	2.11*	-1.15*			
Krugman and Baldwin, (1987) 1977:2-1986:4	2.87*				0.86*

* denotes statistical significance at the .05 level

Table 3.2 (Continued)

COUNTRY	Category				
Author, (Year) Period	Y	PM/PD PM		PD	XR

UNITED STATES (Continued)

Non-Oil (Continued)

Baldwin, (1988) 1983:2-1987:2	2.51*	-2.26*			
Helkie and Hooper, (1988) 1969:1-1984:4	2.11*	-1.15*			
Hooper and Mann, (1989) 1969:1-1984:4	2.07*	-1.13*			
Blecker, (1992) 1977:1-1990:3	2.68*	-0.83*			
Hickok and Hung, (1992) 1967:1-1988:4	2.15*	-1.28*			
Zeitz, (1992) 1980:3-1990:2	2.04*	-0.86*			
Hooper and Marquez, (1993) 1976:3-1992:2	2.50*	-1.03*			
Zeitz and Pemberton, (1993) 1976:1-1990:4	2.48*	-1.14*			
Marquez, (1996) 1952-1992	3.25*	-0.54*			

* denotes statistical significance at the .05 level

Table 3.2 (Continued)

COUNTRY	Category				
Author, (Year) Period	Y	PM/PD PM	PD	XR

UNITED STATES (Continued)

Non-Oil and Computer

Lawrence, (1990) 1976:1-1990:1	1.81*	-0.47*			
Zeitz and Pemberton, (1993) 1976:1-1990:4	2.50*	-0.84*			

Non-Energy

Feldman, (1984) 1970:2-1980:2	1.75*	-1.62*			
Bosworth, (1993) 1970-1990	2.14*	-0.89*			

Non-Crude Materials and Foods

Deyak, et al., (1990) 1958:1-1985:4	2.8785*		-1.3847*	1.4881*	

* denotes statistical significance at the .05 level

**Table 3.3   Import Demand Elasticities by Country
Broad Commodity Categories for Imports**

COUNTRY	Category				
Author, (Year) Period	Y	PM/PD PM		PD	XR
AUSTRALIA					
Basic Metals					
Athukorala and Menon, (1995) 1981:3-1991:2	1.00*	-0.95*			
Chemicals					
Athukorala and Menon, (1995) 1981:3-1991:2	1.56*	-2.10*			
Electrical					
Menon, (1995) 1981:3-1992:2	1.84	-0.41			
Fabricated Metal Products					
Athukorala and Menon, (1995) 1981:3-1991:2	1.00*	-0.39*			
Iron and Steel					
Menon, (1995) 1981:3-1992:2	1.30	-1.30			
Machinery					
Menon, (1995) 1981:3-1992:2	2.07	-0.96			

* denotes statistical significance at the .05 level

Table 3.3 (Continued)

COUNTRY		Category			
Author, (Year) Period	Y	PM/PD PM		PD	XR

AUSTRALIA (Continued)

Manufacturing

Bosworth, (1993) 1970-1990	0.90*	-1.05*			
Athukorala and Menon, (1995) 1981:3-1991:2	1.00*	-0.37*			
Menon, (1995) 1981:3-1992:2	1.87	-0.66			

Metal Manufactures

Menon, (1995) 1981:3-1992:2	1.32	-0.36			

Misc. Manufacturing

Menon, (1995) 1981:3-1992:2	1.66	-0.60			

Non Metallic Minerals

Athukorala and Menon, (1995) 1981:3-1991:2	1.00*	-0.43*			

Other Machinery

Athukorala and Menon, (1995) 1981:3-1991:2	1.00*	-0.37*			

---

* denotes statistical significance at the .05 level

Table 3.3 (Continued)

COUNTRY	Category			
Author, (Year) Period	Y	PM/PD PM	PD	XR
AUSTRALIA (Continued)		**Road Vehicles**		
Menon, (1995) 1981:3-1992:2	1.06	-0.48		
		Transport Equipment		
Athukorala and Menon, (1995) 1981:3-1991:2	1.00*	-1.27*		
		Travel Services		
Moshirian, (1993) 1964-1986	1.5*	-0.50		
AUSTRIA		**Manufacturing**		
Bosworth, (1993) 1970-1990	1.57*	-1.03*		
		Travel Services		
Moshirian, (1993) 1972-1986	1.7*	-1.6*		

* denotes statistical significance at the .05 level

Table 3.3 (Continued)

COUNTRY		Category			
Author, (Year) Period	Y	PM/PD PM		PD	XR
BANGLADESH		**Chemicals**			
Nguyen and Bhuyan, (1977) 1954-1968	1.983*	-0.969			
		Crude Materials			
Nguyen and Bhuyan, (1977) 1954-1968	4.722*	-1.306*			
		Food, Beverages and Tobacco			
Nguyen and Bhuyan, (1977) 1954-1968	5.190*	-0.591*			
		Machinery and Transport			
Nguyen and Bhuyan, (1977) 1954-1968	1.388*	-0.756*			
		Manufacturing			
Nguyen and Bhuyan, (1977) 1954-1968	1.696	-1.185			
		Mineral Fuels			
Nguyen and Bhuyan, (1977) 1954-1968	1.925*	-0.895			

* denotes statistical significance at the .05 level

Table 3.3 (Continued)

COUNTRY		Category			
Author, (Year) Period	Y	PM/PD	PM	PD	XR

BANGLADESH (Continued)

Misc. Manufacturing

Nguyen and Bhuyan, (1977) 1954-1968	1.217*	-0.760			

BELGIUM

Manufacturing

Goldstein and Khan, (1976) 1958:2-1973:4	1.97*	-0.976*			
Krugman, (1989) 1971-1986	1.99*	-0.53*			
Bosworth, (1993) 1970-1990	1.03*	-0.55*			

BRAZIL

Agricultural Products

Zini, (1988) 1970:1-1986:3	1.98*		-0.263*	0.124	

Consumer Durables

Weisskoff, (1979) 1953-1970	2.88*	-0.07			

---

* denotes statistical significance at the .05 level

Table 3.3 (Continued)

COUNTRY		Category			
Author, (Year) Period	Y	PM/PD PM	PD	XR	

BRAZIL (Continued)

Consumer Goods

Weisskoff, (1979) 1953-1970	2.19*	-0.27			

Industrial Goods

Dib, (1981) 1960-1978	0.97*	-1.19*			
Zini, (1988) 1970:1-1986:3	1.19*		-0.558*	0.466*	

Metallic Intermediate Goods

Weisskoff, (1979) 1953-1970	2.75	-0.42*			

Mineral Products

Zini, (1988) 1970:1-1986:3	3.21*		-0.045	0.251*	

Nonmetallic Intermediate Goods

Weisskoff, (1979) 1953-1970	2.01*	-0.41*			

* denotes statistical significance at the .05 level

Table 3.3 (Continued)

COUNTRY	Category				
Author, (Year) Period	Y	PM/PD	PM	PD	XR
CANADA					
		Agricultural Products			
Koo, et al., (1991) 1972-1985	0.27			-0.21	0.29
		Construction Materials			
Yadav, (1977) 1956:1-1973:4	0.455*	-2.518*			
		Food			
Yadav, (1977) 1956:1-1973:4	0.791*	-0.613*			
		Industrial Materials			
Yadav, (1975) 1956:1-1972:4	0.660*	-1.317*			
Yadav, (1977) 1956:1-1973:4	1.049*	-0.812*			
		Industrial Products			
Koo, et al., (1991) 1972-1985	0.76*			-0.63*	0.72*

* denotes statistical significance at the .05 level

Table 3.3 (Continued)

COUNTRY		Category			
Author, (Year) Period	Y	PM/PD PM		PD	XR

CANADA (Continued)

Manufacturing

Akhtar, (1981) 1969-1978	1.0*	-0.9*
Krugman, (1989) 1971-1986	1.66*	-1.45*
Bosworth, (1993) 1970-1990	1.46*	-0.86*

Other Consumer Goods

Yadav, (1977) 1956:1-1973:4	1.513*	-3.176*

Producers Equipment

Yadav, (1975) 1956:1-1972:4	0.984*	-0.869*
Yadav, (1977) 1956:1-1973:4	1.133*	-1.020*

Travel Services

Moshirian, (1993) 1964-1986	1.7*	-0.59*

* denotes statistical significance at the .05 level

Table 3.3 (Continued)

COUNTRY	Category				
Author, (Year) Period	Y	PM/PD	PM	PD	XR
CHILE					
	Capital Goods				
Meller and Cabezas, (1989) 1974:1-1981:4	2.157*	-0.486*			
	Consumer Goods				
Meller and Cabezas, (1989) 1974:1-1981:4	2.737*	-1.459*			
Rojas and Assael, (1994) 1960-1992	3.47*	-0.33			
	Intermediate Goods				
Meller and Cabezas, (1989) 1974:1-1987:4	0.341	-0.444*			
Rojas and Assael, (1994) 1960-1992	1.41*	-0.26*			
DENMARK					
	Manufacturing				
Bosworth, (1993) 1970-1990	1.49*	-0.07			

* denotes statistical significance at the .05 level

Table 3.3 (Continued)

COUNTRY	Category				
Author, (Year) Period	Y	PM/PD	PM	PD	XR
FINLAND					
Consumption Goods					
Aurikko, (1985) 1963:1-1983:4	1.72*	-0.92*			
Fuels and Lubricants					
Aurikko, (1985) 1963:1-1983:4	1.86*	-0.30*			
Investment Goods					
Aurikko, (1985) 1963:1-1983:4	1.33*	-0.73*			
Raw Materials					
Aurikko, (1985) 1963:1-1983:4	1.05*	-0.69*			
Travel Services					
Moshirian, (1993) 1964-1986	2.3*	-1.1*			
FRANCE					
Fuel					
Humphrey, (1976) 1957-1972	1.289*	-0.566*			

* denotes statistical significance at the .05 level

Table 3.3 (Continued)

COUNTRY	Category				
Author, (Year) Period	Y	PM/PD	PM	PD	XR
FRANCE (Continued)					
Manufacturing					
Goldstein and Khan, (1976) 1957:2-1973:4	2.47*	-0.597*			
Humphrey, (1976) 1957-1972	2.300*	-1.034*			
Lawrence, (1987) 1973-1985	2.69*	-1.11*			
Bosworth, (1993) 1970-1990	1.51*	-0.82*			
Travel Services					
Moshirian, (1993) 1964-1986	1.2*	-0.98*			
GERMANY					
Autos					
Lachler, (1985) 1960-1981	1.799*		-0.329	0.062	
Basic Materials					
Humphrey, (1976) 1955-1972	0.579*	-0.400			

* denotes statistical significance at the .05 level

Table 3.3 (Continued)

COUNTRY		Category			
Author, (Year) Period	Y	PM/PD	PM	PD	XR

GERMANY (Continued)

Chemicals

Lachler, (1985) 1960-1981	0.451	-1.009*			

Food, Beverages and Tobacco

Humphrey, (1976) 1955-1972	0.885*	-0.816*			

General Machinery

Lachler, (1985) 1960-1981	1.152*	-2.283			

Iron and Steel

Lachler, (1985) 1960-1981	0.758*		-2.576*	1.431*	

Manufacturing

Goldstein and Khan, (1976) 1957:2-1973:4	2.264*	-0.772*			
Humphrey, (1976) 1955-1972	2.314*	-0.826			
Akhtar and Hilton, (1984) 1974-1981	1.58*	-2.99*			

* denotes statistical significance at the .05 level

Table 3.3 (Continued)

COUNTRY	Category				
Author, (Year) Period	Y	PM/PD	PM	PD	XR

GERMANY (Continued)

Manufacturing (Continued)

Lawrence, (1987) 1971-1986	2.77*	-0.54*			
Krugman, (1989) 1971-1986	2.83*	-0.09			
Bosworth, (1993) 1970-1990	0.82*	-0.91*			

Semi-Manufacturing

Humphrey, (1976) 1955-1972	2.304*	-0.739*			

Travel Services

Moshirian, (1993) 1964-1986	1.4*	-0.42*			

GHANA

Manufacturing and Capital Goods

Quarcoo, (1991) 1967-1983	1.0929*				-0.1293*

---

* denotes statistical significance at the .05 level

Table 3.3 (Continued)

COUNTRY	Category				
Author, (Year) Period	Y	PM/PD	PM	PD	XR

GHANA (Continued)

Raw Material and Intermediate Goods

Quarcoo, (1991) 1967-1983	1.1969*				-0.2451*

GREECE

Chemicals

Hitiris and Petoussis, (1984) 1957:1-1975:4	0.506*	-1.237*			

Industrial Products

Zonzilos, (1991) 1976:1-1986:4	1.293*		-0.810*	0.655*	

Machinery and Transport Equip.

Hitiris and Petoussis, (1984) 1957:1-1975:4	1.657*	-0.801*			

Manufacturing

Hitiris and Petoussis, (1984) 1957:1-1975:4	0.612*	-0.891*			

* denotes statistical significance at the .05 level

Table 3.3 (Continued)

COUNTRY	Category				
Author, (Year) Period	Y	PM/PD	PM	PD	XR
INDIA					
	Chemicals				
Nguyen and Bhuyan, (1977) 1957-1969	1.162*	-0.742*			
Sundararajan and Bhole, (1989) 1960-1983	0.5325*	-0.7127*			
	Crude Materials				
Sundararajan and Bhole, (1989) 1960-1983	0.5959*	-0.1631			
	Food				
Nguyen and Bhuyan,(1977) 1957-1969	3.094*	-2.903*			
	Food and Beverages				
Sundararajan and Bhole, (1989) 1960-1983	1.1046*	-0.1034*			
	Machinery and Transport				
Sundararajan and Bhole, (1989) 1960-1983	0.2238*	-0.2805*			
Nguyen and Bhuyan, (1977) 1957-1969	1.460*	-0.893*			

* denotes statistical significance at the .05 level

Table 3.3 (Continued)

COUNTRY		Category			
Author, (Year) Period	Y	PM/PD PM		PD	XR

INDIA (Continued)

Manufacturing

Nguyen and Bhuyan, (1977) 1957-1969	1.231*	-1.083*			

Manufacturing and Misc.

Sundararajan and Bhole, (1989) 1960-1983	0.2251*	-1.0847*			

Mineral Fuels and Petroleum

Sundararajan and Bhole, (1989) 1960-1983	0.2251*	-1.0847*			

Misc. Manufacturing

Nguyen and Bhuyan, (1977) 1957-1969	2.269*	-1.264*			

IRELAND

Capital Goods

Boylan and Cuddy, (1987) 1953-1976	2.907*	-0.451			

Consumer Goods

Boylan, et al., (1981) 1953-1975	1.73*	-0.17			

* denotes statistical significance at the .05 level

Table 3.3 (Continued)

COUNTRY	Category				
Author, (Year) Period	Y	PM/PD	PM	PD	XR

IRELAND (Continued)

Consumer Goods (Continued)

Boylan and Cuddy, (1987) 1953-1976	0.753*	-1.553*			

Materials

Boylan, et al., (1981) 1953-1975	1.65*	-0.12			
Boylan and Cuddy, (1987) 1953-1976	1.901*	-0.511			

ITALY

Manufacturing

Lawrence, (1987) 1971-1986	2.72*	-2.13*			
Krugman, (1989) 1971-1986	3.65*	-0.68*			
Bosworth, (1993) 1970-1990	1.38*	-1.42*			

Travel Services

Moshirian, (1993) 1964-1986	2.4*	-0.85*			

* denotes statistical significance at the .05 level

Table 3.3 (Continued)

COUNTRY		Category			
Author, (Year) Period	Y	PM/PD PM		PD	XR
JAMAICA		**Agricultural and Industrial** **Raw Materials**			
Gafar, (1981) 1954-1972	0.97*	-0.64*			
Gafar, (1984) 1954-1972	0.28*	-1.58			
		Beverages			
Gafar, (1981) 1954-1972	4.38*	-1.01			
		Capital Goods			
Gafar, (1981) 1954-1972	1.22*	-0.69			
Gafar, (1984) 1954-1972	0.55*	-3.59			
		Chemicals			
Gafar, (1981) 1954-1972	1.15*	-1.11*			
Gafar, (1984) 1954-1972	0.02*	-1.32*			

* denotes statistical significance at the .05 level

Table 3.3 (Continued)

COUNTRY		Category			
Author, (Year) Period	Y	PM/PD PM		PD	XR

JAMAICA (Continued)

Construction Materials

Gafar, (1981) 1954-1972	1.00*	-0.75*	

Consumer Goods

Gafar, (1981) 1954-1972	1.05*	-0.02	
Gafar, (1984) 1954-1972	0.22*	-0.10	

Durables

Gafar, (1981) 1954-1972	1.19*	-0.35*	
Gafar, (1984) 1954-1972	0.03*	-0.41	

Food

Gafar, (1981) 1954-1972	1.04*	-0.58*	
Gafar, (1984) 1954-1972	0.09*	-2.11*	

* denotes statistical significance at the .05 level

Table 3.3 (Continued)

COUNTRY	Category				
Author, (Year) Period	Y	PM/PD PM	PD	XR

JAMAICA (Continued)

Fuels					
Gafar, (1981) 1954-1972	0.94*	-0.19*			
Gafar, (1984) 1954-1972	0.03*	-0.62			
Intermediate Goods					
Gafar, (1981) 1954-1972	0.99*	-0.67			
Gafar, (1984) 1954-1972	0.11*	-3.60			
Machinery					
Gafar, (1981) 1954-1972	1.36*	-0.55			
Gafar, (1984) 1954-1972	0.27*	-1.12			
Non Durables					
Gafar, (1981) 1954-1972	0.89*	-0.67*			
Gafar, (1984) 1954-1972	0.05*	-1.84*			

* denotes statistical significance at the .05 level

Table 3.3 (Continued)

COUNTRY		Category			
Author, (Year) Period	Y	PM/PD PM		PD	XR
JAMAICA (Continued)		Transport Equipment			
Gafar, (1981) 1954-1972	1.38*	-0.08			
Gafar, (1984) 1954-1972	0.08*	-0.04			
JAPAN		Basic Metals			
Lawrence, (1987) 1971-1982	0.37*	-0.17			
		Chemicals			
Lawrence, (1987) 1971-1985	1.43*	-2.17*			
		Electrical Goods			
Lawrence, (1987) 1971-1985	0.90*	-1.40*			
		Food and Drink			
Corker, (1989) 1975-1987	0.293*	-0.358*			

* denotes statistical significance at the .05 level

Table 3.3 (Continued)

COUNTRY	Category				
Author, (Year) Period	Y	PM/PD PM		PD	XR

JAPAN Continued)

Food Products

Lawrence, (1987) 1971-1985	0.08	-0.31			

Fuel

Loopesko and Johnson, (1988) 1974:1-1986:4	1.00	-0.17*			

Industrial Machinery

Lawrence, (1987) 1971-1982	0.54	-1.23*			

Manufacturing

Goldstein and Khan, (1976) 1957:2-1973:4	1.035*	-1.229*			
Akhtar, (1981) 1968-1978	1.4*	-1.5*			
Lawrence, (1987) 1970-1985	1.84*				1.06*
Lawrence, (1987) 1971-1986	1.35*	-1.01*			
Loopesko and Johnson, (1988) 1975:1-1986:4	1.86*	-0.90*			

* denotes statistical significance at the .05 level

Table 3.3 (Continued)

COUNTRY	Category				
Author, (Year) Period	Y	PM/PD	PM	PD	XR
JAPAN (Continued)		**Manufacturing** (Continued)			
Corker, (1989) 1975-1987	0.804*	-0.397*			
Lawrence, (1991) 1971-1985	1.54*	-1.02*			
Petri, (1991) 1975:2-1989:2	1.846*	-0.729*			
Bosworth, (1993) 1970-1990	1.86*	-1.25*			
		Metal Products			
Lawrence, (1987) 1971-1985	0.59	-1.42*			
		Mineral Fuel			
Corker, (1989) 1975-1987	1.044*	-0.107*			
		Motor Vehicles			
Lawrence, (1987) 1971-1985	1.00*	-0.30*			

* denotes statistical significance at the .05 level

Table 3.3 (Continued)

COUNTRY		Category			
Author, (Year) Period	Y	PM/PD PM	PD		XR

JAPAN (Continued)

Non Metallic Minerals

Lawrence, (1987) 1971-1985	0.53*	-1.46*			

Raw Materials

Loopesko and Johnson, (1988) 1974:1-1986:4	0.97*	-0.50*			
Corker, (1989) 1975-1987	1.142*	-0.092			

Travel Services

Moshirian, (1993) 1964-1986	1.8*	-0.56*			

MEXICO

Capital Goods

Salas, (1982) 1961-1979	1.890*	-1.409*			-1.297*
Salas, (1982) 1961-1979	0.589*	-1.501*			-1.242*
Salas, (1988) 1961-1986	0.788*	-1.857*			1.255*

* denotes statistical significance at the .05 level

Table 3.3 (Continued)

COUNTRY		Category			
Author, (Year) Period	Y	PM/PD PM		PD	XR
MEXICO (Continued)		**Consumption Goods**			
Salas, (1982) 1961-1979	0.624*	-3.401*			-1.747
Salas, (1982) 1961-1979	0.624*	-3.401*			-1.748
Salas, (1988) 1961-1979	0.839*	-2.427*			-1.885*
		Intermediate Goods			
Salas, (1982) 1961-1979	0.422*	-2.302*			-1.347
Salas, (1982) 1961-1979	0.422*	-2.297*			-1.341*
Salas, (1988) 1961-1988	0.494*	-1.411*			-1.658*
NETHERLANDS		**Manufacturing**			
Krugman, (1989) 1971-1989	2.66*	-0.22			
Bosworth, (1993) 1970-1990	1.75*	-0.32			

* denotes statistical significance at the .05 level

Table 3.3 (Continued)

COUNTRY		Category			
Author, (Year) Period	Y	PM/PD PM	PD	XR

NETHERLANDS (Continued)

Travel Services

Moshirian, (1993) 1972-1986	1.5*	-0.47*

NIGERIA

Capital Goods

Salehi-Isfahini, (1989) 1963-1979	0.79*	-1.75*

Chemicals

Umo, (1991) 1960-1985	0.743*	-0.450

Crude Materials

Umo, (1991) 1960-1985	0.158	-0.004

Food

Salehi-Isfahini, (1989) 1963-1979	0.05	-1.00*

Intermediate Goods

Salehi-Isfahini, (1989) 1963-1979	0.69*	-1.33*

* denotes statistical significance at the .05 level

Table 3.3 (Continued)

COUNTRY	Category				
Author, (Year) Period	Y	PM/PD	PM	PD	XR

NIGERIA (Continued)

Machinery and Transport

Umo, (1991) 1960-1985	0.752*	-0.168			

Mineral Fuels

Umo, (1991) 1960-1985	0.471*	-0.151*			

Raw Materials

Umo, (1991) 1960-1985	0.652*	-0.139*			

NORWAY

Manufacturing

Goldstein and Khan, (1976) 1958:2-1973:4	0.995*	-0.949*			

PAKISTAN

Animal/Vegetable Fats and Oil

Nguyen and Bhuyan, (1977) 1954-1968	6.119*	-5.076*			
Sarmad and Mahmood, (1987) 1969-1984	2.530*	-0.580*			

* denotes statistical significance at the .05 level

Table 3.3 (Continued)

COUNTRY		Category			
Author, (Year) Period	Y	PM/PD PM		PD	XR

PAKISTAN (Continued)

Chemicals

Nguyen and Bhuyan, (1977) 1954-1968	2.666*	-1.657*	
Sarmad and Mahmood, (1987) 1969-1984	2.020*	-0.720*	
Sarmad, (1989) 1959-1986	1.161*	-0.517*	

Crude Inedible Materials

Sarmad, (1989) 1959-1986	1.247*	-0.517*	

Crude Materials

Nguyen and Bhuyan, (1977) 1954-1968	1.184*	-0.184	
Sarmad and Mahmood, (1987) 1969-1984	1.444*	-0.816*	

Food, Beverages and Tobacco

Nguyen and Bhuyan, (1977) 1954-1968	2.761*	-1.623*	

* denotes statistical significance at the .05 level

Table 3.3 (Continued)

COUNTRY	Category				
Author, (Year) Period	Y	PM/PD	PM	PD	XR
PAKISTAN (Continued)					
Food Products					
Sarmad and Mahmood, (1987) 1969-1984	3.160*	-0.740			
Fuels					
Sarmad and Mahmood, (1987) 1969-1984	0.736*	-0.051			
Sarmad, (1989) 1959-1986	0.447*	-0.433*			
Machinery and Transport					
Nguyen and Bhuyan, (1977) 1954-1968	6.388*	-1.139*			
Sarmad and Mahmood, (1987) 1969-1984	4.140*	-0.450			
Sarmad, (1989) 1959-1986	1.251*	-1.208*			
Manufacturing					
Nguyen and Bhuyan, (1977) 1954-1968	1.899*	-0.875*			
Sarmad, (1989) 1959-1986	0.492*	-0.819*			

* denotes statistical significance at the .05 level

Table 3.3 (Continued)

COUNTRY		Category			
Author, (Year) Period	Y	PM/PD	PM	PD	XR
PAKISTAN (Continued)					
		Mineral Fuels			
Nguyen and Bhuyan, (1977) 1954-1968	2.753*	-1.570*			
		Misc. Manufacturing			
Nguyen and Bhuyan, (1977) 1954-1968	3.986*	-0.920			
Sarmad, (1989) 1959-1986	0.671*	-0.764*			
		Oils and Fats			
Sarmad, (1989) 1959-1986	1.419*	-0.420*			
PHILIPPINES					
		Animal/Vegetable Oil			
Bautista, (1977) 1956-1972	0.58*	-0.15*			
		Beverages and Tobacco			
Bautista, (1977) 1952-1972	1.29*	-0.462*			

* denotes statistical significance at the .05 level

Table 3.3 (Continued)

COUNTRY	Category				
Author, (Year) Period	Y	PM/PD	PM	PD	XR

PHILIPPINES (Continued)

Chemicals

Bautista, (1977) 1954-1972	19.51*	-0.383			

Food

Bautista, (1977) 1952-1972	3.08*	-1.236*			
Bautista, (1978) 1952-1974	1.073*			-1.005*	0.916*

Machinery and Equipment

Bautista, (1977) 1955-1972	13.24*	-0.703*			

Mineral Fuels

Bautista, (1977) 1953-1972	1.02	-1.206*			

Misc. Manufacturing

Bautista, (1977) 1953-1972	1.44*	-0.422*			

* denotes statistical significance at the .05 level

Table 3.3 (Continued)

COUNTRY		Category			
Author, (Year) Period	Y	PM/PD	PM	PD	XR

SOUTH AFRICA

Agriculture

Kahn, (1987) 1974:1-1985:2	0.19*	-0.79*			

Chemicals

Kahn, (1987) 1974:1-1985:2	0.70*	-1.37*			

Machinery and Transport

Kahn, (1987) 1974:1-1985:2	2.96*	-0.14			

Manufacturing

Kahn, (1987) 1974:1-1986:1	0.72*	-0.55*			

SRI LANKA

Consumer Goods

Nguyen and Bhuyan, (1977) 1952-1970	3.094*	-1.769*			

Food and Beverages

Nguyen and Bhuyan, (1977) 1952-1970	0.538*	-0.390			

* denotes statistical significance at the .05 level

Table 3.3 (Continued)

COUNTRY	Category				
Author, (Year) Period	Y	PM/PD	PM	PD	XR

SRI LANKA (Continued)

Intermediate Goods

Nguyen and Bhuyan, (1977) 1955-1970	0.065	-0.313*			

Investment Goods

Nguyen and Bhuyan, (1977) 1955-1970	0.810*	-0.635*			

SWEDEN

Chemicals

Hamilton, (1980) 1960-1975	1.31*	-1.79*			

Leather, Textiles, Clothing

Hamilton, (1980) 1960-1975	0.33*	-1.13*			

Manufacturing

Bosworth, (1993) 1970-1990	1.09*	-1.04*			

Metal Manufactures

Hamilton, (1980) 1960-1975	0.88*	-1.64*			

* denotes statistical significance at the .05 level

Table 3.3 (Continued)

COUNTRY	Category				
Author, (Year) Period	Y	PM/PD	PM	PD	XR

SWEDEN (Continued)

Travel Services

Moshirian, (1993) 1964-1986	2.4*	-0.73			

SWITZERLAND

Travel Services

Moshirian, (1993) 1964-1986	0.97*	-0.53*			

TRINIDAD and TOBAGO

Animal/ Vegetable Fats and Oil

Gafar, (1988) 1967-1984	1.5139*		-0.3319*	0.4537*	

Beverages and Tobacco

Gafar, (1988) 1967-1984	2.1420*		-0.1115	0.0049	

Chemicals

Gafar, (1988) 1967-1984	2.0617*		-0.6521*	0.7219*	

---

* denotes statistical significance at the .05 level

Table 3.3 (Continued)

COUNTRY	Category				
Author, (Year) Period	Y	PM/PD PM		PD	XR

TRINIDAD and TOBAGO (Continued)

Crude Materials except Food

Gafar, (1988) 1967-1984	2.6662*		-0.9901*	1.6880*	

Food

Gafar, (1988) 1967-1984	0.4106*		-0.2802*	0.7005*	

Machinery and Transport Equipment

Gafar, (1988) 1967-1984	1.7883*		-0.4950*	0.8648*	

Misc. Manufactures

Gafar (1988) 1967-1984	2.0232*		-0.6595	1.2789*	

TUNISIA

Grains

Wilde, (1987) 1960-1981	2.451*	-1.572*			

---

* denotes statistical significance at the .05 level

Table 3.3 (Continued)

COUNTRY	Category				
Author, (Year) Period	Y	PM/PD	PM	PD	XR
UNITED KINGDOM					
Finished Manufactures					
Morgan, (1975) 1955-1971	2.76*	-1.30*			
Humphrey, (1976) 1955-1972	4.464*	-0.762*			
Fuel					
Humphrey, (1976) 1955-1972	2.271*	-0.197*			
Manufactures					
Humphrey, (1976) 1955-1972	3.333*	-0.282			
Cuthberson, (1985) 1967:1-1983:4	2.16*	-0.38*			
Lawrence, (1987) 1972-1986	2.47*	-0.61*			
Anderton and Desai, (1988) 1968:1-1986:4	2.70*	-0.42*			
Anderton, et al., (1992) 1967:1-1987:1	1.619*	-0.2113*			

* denotes statistical significance at the .05 level

Table 3.3 (Continued)

COUNTRY	Category				
Author, (Year) Period	Y	PM/PD	PM	PD	XR

UNITED KINGDOM (Continued)

Manufactures (Continued)

Bosworth, (1993) 1970-1990	0.68*	-0.20			

Motor Vehicles

King, (1993) 1980:1-1990:4	0.8815*	-0.0574*			

Semi-Manufactures

Morgan, (1975) 1955-1971	2.41*	-1.48*			
Humphrey, (1976) 1955-1972	1.918*	-0.075			

Travel Services

Moshirian, (1993) 1964-1986	0.71*	-0.66*			

UNITED STATES

Agricultural Goods

Koo, et al., (1991) 1972-1985	0.26			-1.57*	1.96*

* denotes statistical significance at the .05 level

Table 3.3 (Continued)

COUNTRY	Category				
Author, (Year) Period	Y	PM/PD	PM	PD	XR
UNITED STATES (Continued)					
Crude Foods					
Deyak, et al., (1989) 1958:4-1983:4	0.25*	-0.27*			
Crude Materials					
Deyak, et al., (1989) 1958:4-1983:4	1.70	-0.53			
Finished Manufacturing					
Clark, (1977) 1963:1-1973:2	3.63*	-4.72*			
Doroodian, (1987) 1961-1979	3.59*	-0.957*			
Deyak, et al., (1989) 1958:4-1983:4	3.09*	-1.00*			
Sawyer and Sprinkle, (1997) 1958:1-1987:4	3.7726*		-3.2281*	3.3827*	2.4370*
Food Products					
Lawrence, (1987) 1971-1985	1.13*	-0.72*			

* denotes statistical significance at the .05 level

Table 3.3 (Continued)

COUNTRY	Category				
Author, (Year) Period	Y	PM/PD	PM	PD	XR
UNITED STATES (Continued)					
Industrial Materials					
Clark, (1977) 1966:1-1973:2	0.96*	-1.25*			
Koo, et al., (1991) 1972-1985	0.64*			-0.88*	1.01*
Manufactured Foods					
Deyak, et al, (1989). 1958:4-1983:4	1.24*	-0.29*			
Manufacturing					
Goldstein and Khan, (1976) 1957:2-1973:4	2.896*	-0.477			
Lawrence, (1978) 1962:2-1977:2	2.17*	-1.52*			
Akhtar, (1981) 1968-1978	4.1*	-3.5*			
Akhtar and Hilton, (1984) 1974-1981	2.03*	-2.44*			
Lawrence, (1987) 1971-1986	3.36*	-1.95*			

* denotes statistical significance at the .05 level

Table 3.3 (Continued)

COUNTRY	Category			
Author, (Year) Period	Y	PM/PD PM	PD	XR

UNITED STATES (Continued)

Manufacturing (Continued)

Kim, (1992) 1975:1-1989:4	2.83*	-1.11*		
Bosworth, (1993) 1970-1990	1.25*	-0.93		

Motor Vehicles

Lawrence, (1987) 1971-1985	3.71*	-1.42*		

Nondurable Consumer Goods

Clarida, (1994) 1967:2-1990:2	2.15*	-0.95*		

Semi-Finished Manufacturing

Deyak, et al., (1989) 1958:4-1983:4	1.80*	-0.84*		

VENEZUELA

Agricultural Products

Khan, (1975) 1953-1972	1.362*	-1.176*		

* denotes statistical significance at the .05 level

Table 3.3 (Continued)

COUNTRY	Category				
Author, (Year) Period	Y	PM/PD	PM	PD	XR

VENEZUELA (Continued)

Chemicals

Khan, (1975) 1953-1972	0.664*	-1.277*			
Melo and Vogt, (1984) 1962-1979	1.651*	-0.456			

Food

Melo and Vogt, (1984) 1962-1979	0.5845*	-2.041*			

Machinery and Transport

Khan, (1975) 1953-1972	0.557*	-0.765			
Melo and Vogt, (1984) 1962-1979	2.734*	-1.318*			

Manufacturing

Melo and Vogt, (1984) 1962-1979	0.522*	-0.207			

Tobacco and Beverages

Khan, (1975) 1953-1972	1.969*	-1.033			

* denotes statistical significance at the .05 level

Table 3.3 (Continued)

COUNTRY		Category			
Author, (Year) Period	Y	PM/PD PM		PD	XR

VENEZUELA (Continued)

Tobacco and Beverages (Continued)

	Y	PM/PD		
Melo and Vogt, (1984) 1962-1979	1.773*	-2.324*		

---

* denotes statistical significance at the .05 level

4 The Demand for Exports

Before considering the export elasticities contained in Tables 4.1 through 4.3, some explanatory notes concerning what is covered and not covered is in order. The estimates begin with studies published roughly from 1976 to the most recently available estimates. The survey by Stern, Francis, and Schumacher (1976) covers studies published through 1975. Thus, 1976 is a convenient point of departure. Our discussion of the estimation of export demand elasticities in Chapter 2 implies that some types of export demand elasticities are not presented in the following tables. As we indicated in that chapter, the standard formulation for estimating import demand can be expressed in one of three equations.

The traditional approach to estimating the demand for exports relates changes in the quantity of exports (X) to changes in income and relative prices.

$$X = f(\overset{+}{YF}, \overset{-}{PX/PF}) \tag{4.1}$$

The algebraic signs above the variables indicate the expected signs of the first partial derivative of the function with respect to each of the arguments. The variables are foreign income (YF) usually expressed as real GDP or real GNP; the price of exports (PX) usually an export unit value index; and domestic prices in the foreign country (PF) usually expressed as the wholesale price index. Often both foreign

117

income and foreign prices are a weighted average of a country's trading partners.

The second approach to estimating the demand for exports employs a split-price specification as opposed to the price ratio contained in equation 4.1. This formulation relates changes in the quantity of exports (X) to changes in income and prices separately.

$$\overset{+ \quad - \quad +}{X = f(YF, PX, PF)} \qquad (4.2)$$

Where the variables are defined as above. This specification has the advantage of allowing differential responses in export volumes to changes in international prices versus domestic prices. This could be critical in analyzing changes in exports resulting from change in exchange rate or domestic trade barriers where the price changes would be solely in the exported price.

A final formulation of the demand for exports involves the decomposition of the exported price into changes in domestic prices (PX) and changes in the exchange rate (XR). The specification of the demand for exports can be represented by:

$$\overset{+ \quad - \quad + \quad -/+}{X = f(YF, PX, PF, XR)} \qquad (4.3)$$

Where PX in this formulation represents the price of exports expressed in domestic currency separate from the exchange rate, XR. The advantage of this specification is that it allows one to view how exports respond to changes in exchange rate as a separate issue. The algebraic sign associated with XR depends on the way the exchange rate is defined. The exchange rate variable will be positive if the exchange rate is defined in terms of local currency per unit of foreign currency, and negative if defined in terms of foreign currency per unit of domestic currency.

Equations 4.1 through 4.3 represent the "standard" view of these relationships, however, several of the estimated export demand functions contained in the following tables do not use these standard views. In several cases, the export demand equation has been estimated without price variables and only the exchange rate, or with a price ratio and an exchange rate.

In addition, estimates of export demand elasticities which produced a "wrong" sign on any of the variables were omitted from the following tables. We viewed a wrong sign on any coefficient as a plausible indication of specification error and/or difficulties with the sample period data. As a result, such empirical estimates were omitted. The omitting of these estimates did not result in the deletion of a large number of studies, but one should be aware of this aspect of the results reported in the tables.

Tables 4.1 through 4.3 provide a total of 321 estimates of the demand for exports, and each of the tables is structured as follows. The first column contains the name(s) of the author(s) followed by the year of publication in parentheses. Below the author(s) name(s), the time period utilized to estimate the parameters is reported. If no numbers appear after the year, the data employed in the analysis was annual data. In the second column, estimates of the income elasticity are presented. For all parameter estimates a * denotes statistical significance at the .05 level of significance or higher. The results of the price-ratio specification are given in the third column. Columns four, five, and six present the estimated elasticities for export prices (PX), foreign prices (PF), and the exchange rate (XR) separately. Thus, it is relatively simple to determine the specification which was employed in the study.

Table 4.1 contains estimates of the demand for aggregate or total merchandise exports and estimates for the demand for exported goods and services together. In total, Table 4.1 presents a total of 203 estimates covering 54 countries. Three broad conclusions stand out. First, the primary specification used in estimating export demand is the price ratio specification (Equation 4.1). The split-price specification is the second most commonly used specification (Equation 4.2). The specification employing both split prices and the exchange rate is seldom used (Equation 4.3). Second, the estimated income elasticities of demand generally fall in the range of 1 to 2. Third, the estimated price elasticities of demand are generally small and are in the range of 0 to -1.

Since the quantity of exported oil, energy products, agricultural products, crude materials, etc. may be less responsive to changes in income and relative prices, it is common to estimate the elasticities for total exports minus various offending categories. Table 4.2 contains estimates of the demand for total exports minus various sub-categories of imports. In total, Table 4.2 presents a total of 23 estimates covering 16 countries.

Lastly, Table 4.3 presents estimates of the demand for exports for rather broad product categories. In total, Table 4.3 presents at total of 95 estimates covering 28 countries. It is import to note at this point that further degrees and types of disaggregation are available but not include in the following tables.

Estimates are available for very narrowly defined product categories. Studies in the area include Hossain (1993), Nguyen and Bhuyan (1977), Krinsky (1983) Joseph (1992), Lucas (1988), deMelo, et al. (1995), Conway (1987), Haniotis (1990), Citrin (1985) and Moshirian (1993). It is also possible to obtain estimates of total country exports by country. Studies analyzing exports of a particular country by country include Aurikko (1985), Bini-Smaghi (1991) Chan and Wong (1985), Chou and Shih (1988), O'Neill and Ross (1991), Kumar and Dhawan (1991), Marquez (1991), Bergstrand (1987), Haynes et al. (1986) and Craig (1986). A final category of export demand elasticities not included in the tables are exports by product and by country/region. Studies in this area include Muscatelli, et al. (1995), Chou and Shih (1988), Babula (1987), Cima (1986), and Truett and Truett (1992).

**Table 4.1   Export Demand Elasticities by Country
Total Merchandise Exports**

COUNTRY	Category				
Author, (Year) Period	YF	PX/PF	PX	PF	XR
ARGENTINA		**Total Exports**			
Agarwal, (1984) 1970-1978	1.78*	-0.50*			-0.73*
Faini, et al., (1992) 1967-1983	0.57*	-1.99			
AUSTRALIA		**Goods and Services**			
Andersen, (1993) 1960-1990	1.30	-0.32			
		Total Exports			
Warner and Kreinin, (1983) 1971:3-1978:4	0.41*		-0.17	0.36	-0.57*
Bailey, et al, (1987) 1975:1-1985:3	0.99*	-0.38			
Katayama, et al., (1987) 1970:1-1980:4	0.563*	-0.218			
Bahmani-O. and Niroomand, (1998) 1960-1992	1.91*	-0.12			

* denotes statistical significance at the .05 level

Table 4.1 (Continued)

COUNTRY	Category				
Author, (Year) Period	YF	PX/PF	PX	PF	XR
AUSTRIA		Goods and Services			
Andersen, (1993) 1960-1990	2.30	-0.53			
		Total Exports			
Warner and Kreinin, (1983) 1971:3-1978:4	1.39*		-0.20	1.41*	-2.16*
Bahmani-O. and Niroomand, (1998) 1960-1992	1.43*	-1.14*			
BANGLADESH		Total Exports			
Nguyen and Bhuyan, (1977) 1954-1968	0.848*	-0.337*			
Kabir, (1988) 1973:1-1984:4	0.37*		-0.26	0.34*	0.61*
Hossain, (1993) 1974:1-1985:4	1.376*	-0.828*			

* denotes statistical significance at the .05 level

Table 4.1 (Continued)

COUNTRY	Category				
Author, (Year) Period	YF	PX/PF PX		PF	XR
BELGIUM		**Goods and Services**			
Andersen, (1993) 1960-1990	1.89	-0.09			
		Total Exports			
Goldstein and Khan, (1978) 1955:1-1970:4	1.683*	-1.572*			
Warner and Kreinin, (1983) 1971:3-1978:4	1.38*		-0.41	0.90	-0.88
Yang, (1987) 1960-1972	2.04*	-1.77*			
Bahmani-O. and Niroomand, (1998) 1960-1992	1.82*	-0.10*			
BRAZIL		**Total Exports**			
Lemgruber, (1976) 1965-1974	1.97*	-0.41*			
Agarwal, (1984) 1969-1978	0.253*	-1.23*			-0.56*
Bahmani-Oskooee, (1986) 1974:1-1980:4	0.007	-0.151			

* denotes statistical significance at the .05 level

Table 4.1 (Continued)

COUNTRY	Category				
Author, (Year) Period	YF	PX/PF	PX	PF	XR

BRAZIL (Continued)

Total Exports (Continued)

	YF	PX/PF	PX	PF	XR
Zini, (1988) 1970:1-1986:3	0.690*		-0.171*	0.131	
Faini, et al., (1992) 1967-1983	0.60*	-1.51*			

BURKINA FASO

Total Exports

	YF	PX/PF	PX	PF	XR
Arize, (1987) 1960-1982	0.13	-0.90*			
Arize, (1988) 1960-1982	0.30	-2.1*			

CANADA

Goods and Services

	YF	PX/PF	PX	PF	XR
Andersen, (1993) 1960-1990	1.96	-0.18			

Total Exports

	YF	PX/PF	PX	PF	XR
Wilson and Tackas, (1979) 1957-1971	0.584*		-0.204	4.821	-0.204

* denotes statistical significance at the .05 level

Table 4.1 (Continued)

COUNTRY	Category				
Author, (Year) Period	YF	PX/PF	PX	PF	XR

CANADA (Continued)

Total Exports (Continued)

Witte, (1981) 1973-1978	1.030*		-0.923*		0.434*
Warner and Kreinin, (1983) 1971:3-1978:4	1.36*		-1.37*	1.35*	-0.23
Bailey, et al, (1986) 1973:1-1984:3	1.38*	-0.53*			
Bailey, et al, (1987) 1975:1-1985:3	1.38*	-1.12*			
Katayama, (1987) 1970:1-1980:4	1.001*	-1.337*			
Bahmani-O. and Niroomand, (1998) 1960-1992	1.85*	-0.12*			

CHILE

Total Exports

Faini, et al., (1992) 1967-1983	0.49*	-0.33*			

* denotes statistical significance at the .05 level

Table 4.1 (Continued)

COUNTRY	Category				
Author, (Year) Period	YF	PX/PF	PX	PF	XR
COLOMBIA		Total Exports			
Agarwal, (1984) 1970-1979	1.30*	-0.57*			-1.23*
Faini, et al., (1992) 1967-1983	2.08*	-2.38*			
COTE D' IVOIRE		Total Exports			
Arize, (1987) 1960-1982	0.37		-0.82	0.64*	
Arize, (1988) 1960-1982	0.37		-0.82	0.64*	
Tegene, (1989) 1975:1-1985:4	0.24*	-0.60*			-0.99*
Tegene, (1990) 1973:1-1985:4	0.15	-0.44*			
CYPRUS		Total Exports			
Asseery and Perdikis, (1991) 1960-1987	1.17*	-0.54*			

* denotes statistical significance at the .05 level

Table 4.1 (Continued)

COUNTRY		Category				
Author, (Year) Period	YF	PX/PF	PX		PF	XR
DENMARK		**Goods and Services**				
Andersen, (1993) 1960-1990	1.52	-0.41				
		Total Exports				
Bahmani-O. and Niroomand, (1998) 1960-1992	0.51	-0.93*				
ECUADOR		**Total Exports**				
Agarwal, (1984) 1970-1978	0.86*	-0.34*				-0.98
Faini, et al., (1992) 1967-1983	0.89*	-0.90*				
ETHIOPIA		**Total Exports**				
Tegene, (1989) 1973:1-1985:4	0.13	-0.87*				-0.46
Tegene, (1990) 1973:1-1985:4	0.16	-0.53*				

* denotes statistical significance at the .05 level

Table 4.1 (Continued)

COUNTRY	Category				
Author, (Year) Period	YF	PX/PF	PX	PF	XR
FINLAND		**Goods and Services**			
Andersen, (1993) 1960-1990	1.80	-0.23			
		Total Exports			
Warner and Kreinin, (1983) 1971:3-1978:4	0.40		-1.21	1.76	-1.87*
Agarwal, (1984) 1970-1979	0.56*	-0.987*			-0.765*
Bahmani-O. and Niroomand, (1998) 1960-1992	1.64*	-0.60*			
FRANCE		**Goods and Services**			
Andersen, (1993) 1960-1990	2.25	-0.18			
		Total Exports			
Goldstein and Khan, (1978) 1955-1970	1.693*	-1.334*			
Wilson and Tackas, (1979) 1957-1971	2.138*		-0.399	2.976	-0.393

* denotes statistical significance at the .05 level

Table 4.1 (Continued)

COUNTRY	Category				
Author, (Year) Period	YF	PX/PF	PX	PF	XR

FRANCE (Continued)

Total Exports (Continued)

Warner and Kreinin, (1983) 1971:3-1978:4	0.46		-1.46	1.84	-1.09
Bailey, et al., (1986) 1973:1-1984:3	1.37*	-0.40*			
Katayama, et al., (1987) 1970:1-1980:4	1.675*	-2.772*			
Yang, (1987) 1960-1972	2.01*	-1.59*			

GERMANY

Goods and Services

Andersen, (1993) 1960-1990	1.86	-0.49			

Total Exports

Goldstein and Khan, (1978) 1955-1970	1.805*	-0.831*			
Wilson and Tackas, (1979) 1957-1971	1.108*		-1.874	5.483	-1.869
Warner and Kreinin, (1983) 1971:3-1978:4	0.63*		-4.98*	5.26*	-3.93*

* denotes statistical significance at the .05 level

Table 4.1 (Continued)

COUNTRY Author, (Year) Period	Category				
	YF	PX/PF	PX	PF	XR
GERMANY (Continued) **Total Exports** (Continued)					
Bailey, et al., (1986) 1973:1-1984:3	1.25*	-0.36*			
Bailey, et al., (1987) 1975:1-1985:3	1.18*	-0.41*			
Katayama, et al., (1987) 1970:1-1980:4	1.004*	-0.558*			
Yang, (1987) 1960-1972	1.98*	-1.67*			
Moller and Jarchow, (1990) 1976:1-1986:4	1.2*	-1.3*			
Kroner and Lastrapes, (1993) 1973:2-1990:4	0.2774*	-0.2268*			
GHANA **Total Exports**					
Faini, et al., (1992) 1967-1983	4.01*	-3.37*			

* denotes statistical significance at the .05 level

Table 4.1 (Continued)

COUNTRY	Category				
Author, (Year) Period	YF	PX/PF	PX	PF	XR
GREECE		**Total Exports**			
Bahmani-Oskooee, (1986) 1973:1-1980:4	0.217	-0.247			-0.797
Balassa, et al., (1989) 1960-1978	2.44*	-1.01			
Faini, et al., (1992) 1967-1983	0.44*	-0.79*			
INDIA		**Total Exports**			
Nguyen and Bhuyan, (1977) 1955-1970	1.427*	-0.437*			
Agarwal, (1984) 1970-1979	3.54*	-1.98*			-1.05*
Bahmani-Oskooee, (1986) 1973:1-1979:3	0.433	-2.579			-0.7603
Pradhan, (1988) 1970-1984	0.427*	-0.401*			-1.066*
Arize, (1990) 1973:1-1985:4	0.631*	-0.87*			

* denotes statistical significance at the .05 level

Table 4.1 (Continued)

COUNTRY	Category				
Author, (Year) **Period**	**YF**	**PX/PF**	**PX**	**PF**	**XR**
INDIA (Continued)		Total Exports (Continued)			
Faini, et al., (1992) 1967-1983	0.52*	-0.80*			
Koshal, et al., (1992) 1960-1986	1.3142*		-0.9523*	0.9523*	
INDONESIA		**Total Exports**			
Arize, (1990) 1973:1-1985:4	0.09		-0.087*	0.253*	
ISRAEL		**Total Exports**			
Bahmani-Oskooee, (1986) 1973:1-1980:4	0.151*	-0.648			-0.0302
ITALY		**Goods and Services**			
Andersen, (1993) 1960-1990	2.08	-0.21			

* denotes statistical significance at the .05 level

Table 4.1 (Continued)

COUNTRY	Category				
Author, (Year) Period	YF	PX/PF	PX	PF	XR

ITALY (Continued)

Total Exports

	YF	PX/PF	PX	PF	XR
Goldstein and Khan, (1978) 1955-1970	1.964*	-3.290*			
Warner and Kreinin, (1983) 1971:3-1978:4	0.81*		-0.59	0.74	-1.08
Bailey, et al., (1986) 1973:1-1984:3	1.72*	-0.83*			
Bailey, et al., (1987) 1975:1-1985:3	1.34*	-0.90*			
Yang, (1987) 1960-1972	3.02*	-1.42*			
Bahmani-O. and Niroomand, (1998) 1960-1992	1.78*	-0.24*			

JAPAN

Goods and Services

	YF	PX/PF	PX	PF	XR
Andersen, (1993) 1960-1990	3.82	-0.75			

Total Exports

	YF	PX/PF	PX	PF	XR
Goldstein and Khan, (1978) 1955-1970	1.964*	-3.290*			

* denotes statistical significance at the .05 level

Table 4.1 (Continued)

COUNTRY	Category				
Author, (Year) Period	YF	PX/PF	PX	PF	XR
JAPAN (Continued)					
		Total Exports (Continued)			
Wilson and Tackas, (1979) 1957:1-1971:4	0.864		-11.676	4.905	-11.677
Warner and Kreinin, (1983) 1971:3-1978:4	1.00*		-0.30	1.10*	-0.87
Bailey, et al., (1986) 1973:1-1984:3	1.64*	-1.46*			
Craig, (1986) 1961:3-1985:4	3.57*	-1.14*			
Bailey, et al., (1987) 1975:1-1985:3	1.70*	-1.39*			
Lawrence, (1987) 1970-1985	1.48*				-0.91*
Yang, (1987) 1960-1972	3.54*	-2.65*			
Loopesko and Johnson, (1988) 1970:1-1986:1	1.60*	-1.14*			
Corker, (1989) 1975-1987	0.689*	-0.367*			
Noland, (1989) 1970:1-1985:4	1.36*	-0.41*			

* denotes statistical significance at the .05 level

Table 4.1 (Continued)

COUNTRY	Category				
Author, (Year) Period	YF	PX/PF	PX	PF	XR

JAPAN (Continued)

Total Exports (Continued)

Deyak, et al., (1993) 1958:1-1985:4	2.3020*		-4.8033	5.4736*	-5.6482*
Hooper and Marquez, (1993) 1976:2-1992:2	1.06*	-0.80			
Kroner and Lastrapes, (1993) 1973:2-1990:4	1.1366*	-0.5003			
Ceglowski, (1997) 1976:1-1993:4	1.64*	-1.71*			
Bahmani-O. and Niroomand, (1998) 1960-1992	1.22*	-0.49*			

KENYA

Total Exports

Tegene, (1989) 1973:1-1985:4	0.122	-3.08*			-0.055
Tegene, (1990) 1973:1-1985:4	0.62	-0.67*			

* denotes statistical significance at the .05 level

Table 4.1 (Continued)

COUNTRY Author, (Year) Period	Category				
	YF	PX/PF	PX	PF	XR
KOREA		Total Exports			
Agarwal, (1984) 1970-1978	1.123*	-1.09*			-0.82*
Bahmani-Oskooee, (1986) 1973:1-1980:4	0.337	-0.4271*			0.1327*
Katayama, et al., (1987) 1970:1-1980:4	2.325*	-3.360*			
Balassa, et al., (1989) 1965-1979	5.339*	-1.068*			
Moreno, (1989) 1974:1-1989:4	2.84*	-0.72*			
Arize, (1990) 1973:1-1985:4	0.417*	-1.789*			
Athukorala and Riedel, (1991) 1977:1-1988:4	4.12*	-0.48*			
Faini, et al., (1992) 1967-1983	1.30*	-1.24*			
Bahmani-O. and Niroomand, (1998) 1960-1992	3.37*	-1.52*			

* denotes statistical significance at the .05 level

Table 4.1 (Continued)

COUNTRY Author, (Year) Period	Category				
	YF	PX/PF	PX	PF	XR
MALAWI		Total Exports			
Arize, (1987) 1960-1982	1.99*		-0.48*	2.0*	
Arize, (1988) 1960-1982	1.99*		-0.48*	2.08*	
Tegene, (1989) 1973:1-1985:4	0.021	-1.25*			-0.16*
Tegene, (1990) 1973:1-1985:4	0.13*	-0.82*			
MALAYSIA		Total Exports			
Arize, (1990) 1973:1-1985:4	0.111	-0.146*			
Faini, et al., (1992) 1967-1983	1.46*	-4.00*			
MAURITIUS		Total Exports			
Tegene, (1990) 1973:1-1985:4	0.37*	-0.41*			

* denotes statistical significance at the .05 level

Table 4.1 (Continued)

COUNTRY	Category				
Author, (Year) Period	YF	PX/PF	PX	PF	XR
MAURITIUS (Continued)		**Total Exports** (Continued)			
Bahmani-O. and Niroomand, (1998) 1960-1992	3.53*	-0.86*			
MEXICO		**Total Exports**			
Agarwal, (1984) 1970-1977	0.58*	-0.87*			10.87*
Faini, et al., (1992) 1967-1983	0.93*	-0.85			
MOROCCO		**Total Exports**			
Arize, (1987) 1960-1982	0.18		-0.583*	0.82*	
Arize, (1988) 1960-1982	0.18		-0.82*	1.12*	
Faini, et al., (1992) 1967-1983	1.0*	-1.17*			

* denotes statistical significance at the .05 level

Table 4.1 (Continued)

COUNTRY	Category				
Author, (Year) Period	YF	PX/PF	PX	PF	XR
NETHERLANDS					
Goods and Services					
Andersen, (1993) 1960-1990	1.95	-0.08			
Total Exports					
Goldstein and Khan, (1978) 1955-1970	1.905*	-2.728*			
Warner and Kreinin, (1983) 1971:3-1978:4	1.19*		-1.41	2.72*	-2.72*
Bailey, et al., (1987) 1975:1-1985:3	1.13*	-0.98*			
Yang, (1987) 1960-1972	2.22*	-2.41*			
Bahmani-O. and Niroomand, (1998) 1960-1992	1.44*	-0.27*			
NEW ZEALAND					
Total Exports					
Bailey, et al., (1987) 1975:1-1985:3	2.12*	-0.60			
Joumard and Reisen, (1992) 1980:1-1990:3	1.15*				-0.79*

* denotes statistical significance at the .05 level

Table 4.1 (Continued)

COUNTRY	Category				
Author, (Year) Period	YF	PX/PF	PX	PF	XR

NIGERIA

Total Exports

Arize, (1988) 1953-1981	1.73*		-0.88*	0.75*	

NORWAY

Total Exports

Warner and Kreinin, (1983) 1971:3-1978:4	0.07		-1.53*	2.60*	-2.58*

PAKISTAN

Total Exports

Nguyen and Bhuyan, (1977) 1954-1968	5.085*	-3.924*			
Arize, (1990) 1973:1-1985:4	1.211*		-0.591*	0.621*	
Faini, et al., (1992) 1967-1983	1.28	-1.05*			

PERU

Total Exports

Agarwal, (1984) 1970-1979	0.53*	-1.56*			-2.38*

* denotes statistical significance at the .05 level

Table 4.1 (Continued)

COUNTRY	Category				
Author, (Year) Period	YF	PX/PF	PX	PF	XR
PERU (Continued)		**Total Exports** (Continued)			
Faini, et al., (1992) 1967-1983	0.51*	-3.00*			
PHILIPPINES		**Total Exports**			
Agarwal, (1984) 1970-1978	0.86	-0.13			-5.68*
Bahmani-O. and Niroomand, (1998) 1960-1992	0.81*	-1.56*			
SINGAPORE		**Total Exports**			
Faini, et al., (1992) 1967-1983	0.64*	-0.75*			
SOUTH AFRICA		**Total Exports**			
Bahmani-Oskooee, (1986) 1973:1-1980:4	0.458*	-1.1276*			0.02339
Smit, (1991) 1974-1988	0.51*	-0.63*			

* denotes statistical significance at the .05 level

Table 4.1 (Continued)

COUNTRY		Category				
Author, (Year) Period	YF	PX/PF	PX	PF	XR	

SOUTH AFRICA (Continued)

Total Exports (Continued)

Bahmani-O. and Niroomand, (1998) 1960-1992	1.32*	-0.98*				

SPAIN

Goods and Services

Andersen, (1993) 1960-1990	2.94	-0.53				

Total Exports

Warner and Kreinin, (1983) 1971:3-1979:4	0.25		-0.69	1.51*	-1.16*	
Bahmani-O. and Niroomand, (1998) 1960-1992	2.88*	-0.71*				

SRI LANKA

Total Exports

Nguyen and Bhuyan, (1977) 1955-1970	0.494*	-0.209				

* denotes statistical significance at the .05 level

Table 4.1 (Continued)

COUNTRY		Category			
Author, (Year) Period	YF	PX/PF PX		PF	XR
SWEDEN		**Goods and Services**			
Andersen, (1993) 1960-1990	1.55	-0.45			
		Total Exports			
Warner and Kreinin, (1983) 1971:3-1978:4	0.08		-2.57	3.16*	-1.71*
Bahmani-O. and Niroomand, (1998) 1960-1992	1.02*	-0.67*			
SWITZERLAND		**Goods and Services**			
Andersen, (1993) 1960-1990	1.49	-0.09			
		Total Exports			
Warner and Kreinin, (1983) 1971:3-1978:4	1.40*		-2.32*	2.28*	-1.63*

* denotes statistical significance at the .05 level

Table 4.1 (Continued)

COUNTRY Author, (Year) Period	Category				
	YF	PX/PF	PX	PF	XR
SYRIA		Total Exports			
Agarwal, (1984) 1969-1978	0.43*	-1.09*			-2.56*
TAIWAN		Total Exports			
Agarwal, (1984) 1970-1978	0.67*	-0.65*			-4.53*
Moreno, (1989) 1974:1-1987:4	2.87*	-0.78*			
THAILAND		Total Exports			
Bahmani-Oskooee, (1986) 1973:1-1980:4	0.123	-2.435*			0.0897*
Arize, (1990) 1973:1-1985:4	0.552*		-0.468*	0.432*	
Faini, et al., (1992) 1967-1983	2.55*	-1.70*			

* denotes statistical significance at the .05 level

Table 4.1 (Continued)

COUNTRY	Category				
Author, (Year) Period	YF	PX/PF	PX	PF	XR
TUNISIA		Total Exports			
Arize, (1987) 1960-1982	1.54*		-0.11	1.58*	
Arize, (1988) 1960-1982	1.54*		-0.11	1.58*	
Tegene, (1989) 1973:1-1985:4	0.034		-0.51*	0.086*	
Tegene, (1990) 1973:1-1985:4	0.71	-0.45*			
Faini, et al., (1992) 1967-1983	1.08*	-0.76*			
Bahmani-O. and Niroomand, (1998) 1960-1992	1.02*	-1.14*			
TURKEY		Total Exports			
Tansel and Togan, (1987) 1960-1985	0.6795*	-1.0487*			
Faini, et al., (1992) 1967-1983	1.22*	-3.32*			

* denotes statistical significance at the .05 level

Table 4.1 (Continued)

COUNTRY	Category				
Author, (Year) Period	YF	PX/PF	PX	PF	XR
UNITED KINGDOM		**Goods and Services**			
Andersen, (1993) 1960-1990	1.42	-0.12			
		Total Exports			
Goldstein and Khan, (1978) 1955-1970	0.918*	-1.323*			
Wilson and Tackas, (1979) 1957-1971	1.751*		-0.372	1.778	-0.375
Dunlevy, (1980) 1957-1980	0.59*	-0.40*			
Warner and Kreinin, (1983) 1971:3-1978:4	0.51*		-0.86*	0.76*	-1.70*
Bailey, et al., (1986) 1973:1-1984:3	1.30*	-0.25*			
Bailey, et al., (1987) 1975:1-1985:3	1.69*	-0.70*			
Katayama, et al., (1987) 1970:1-1980:4	1.336	-2.057*			
Yang, (1987) 1960-1972	1.16*	-1.13*			

* denotes statistical significance at the .05 level

Table 4.1 (Continued)

COUNTRY	Category				
Author, (Year) Period	YF	PX/PF	PX	PF	XR

UNITED KINGDOM (Continued)

Total Exports (Continued)

Kroner and Lastrapes, (1993) 1973:2-1990:4	0.2791*	-0.012			
Arize, (1996) 1973:2-1992:4	1.51*		-0.39*	0.52*	
Bahmani-O. and Niroomand, (1998) 1960-1992	1.41*	-0.36			

UNITED STATES

Goods and Services

Andersen, (1993) 1960-1990	1.34	-0.43			

Total Exports

Goldstein and Khan, (1978) 1955:1-1970:4	1.010*	-2.319*			
Stern, et al, (1979). 1956:3-1976:2	0.374*		-0.204	1.271*	-1.068*
Wilson and Tackas, (1979) 1957:1-1971:4	2.151*		-3.309	4.185	-3.310
Dunlevy, (1980) 1957:1-1975:4	0.78*	-0.56*			

* denotes statistical significance at the .05 level

Table 4.1 (Continued)

COUNTRY	Category				
Author, (Year) Period	YF	PX/PF	PX	PF	XR

UNITED STATES (Continued)

Total Exports (Continued)

Haynes and Stone, (1982) 1955:1-1969:4	0.83*	-0.07			
Haynes and Stone, (1983) 1955:1-1979:4	0.74*		-0.77*	1.10*	
Warner and Kreinin (1983) 1971:3-1978:4	1.26*		-0.55	0.86*	-1.50*
Haynes and Stone, (1984) 1955:1-1969:4	0.96*		-1.73*	0.03*	
Bailey, et al., (1986) 1973:1-1984:3	1.08*	-0.59*			
Bailey, et al., (1987) 1975:1-1985:3	1.07*	-0.66*			
Katayama, et al., (1987) 1970:1-1980:4	0.489	-1.043			
Yang, (1987) 1960-1972	2.05*	-2.27*			
Di Liberto, (1988) 1962:1-1980:4	1.32*	-0.55*			
Moffett, (1989) 1967:1-1987:4	1.12*		-0.79*	0.81*	

* denotes statistical significance at the .05 level

Table 4.1 (Continued)

COUNTRY	Category				
Author, (Year) Period	YF	PX/PF	PX	PF	XR

UNITED STATES (Continued)

Total Exports (Continued)

Bahmani-Oskooee, (1991) 1973:1-1988:4	1.2325*				0.3049*
Moreno, (1991) 1972:4-1987:4	1.78*	-0.41*			
Deyak, et al., (1993) 1958:1-1985:4	0.8699*		-0.7736*	0.7749*	-0.8703*
Hooper and Marquez, (1993) 1972:2-1992:2	1.00*	-1.01*			
Arize, (1995) 1973:2-1991:3	1.02*	-0.88*			
Bahmani-O. and Niroomand, (1998) 1960-1992	0.72	-1.60*			

VENEZUELA

Total Exports

Agarwal, (1984) 1970-1978	0.89*	-0.98*			-6.98
Faini, et al., (1992) 1967-1983	1.0*	-1.89*			

* denotes statistical significance at the .05 level

Table 4.1 (Continued)

COUNTRY	Category				
Author, (Year) **Period**	**YF**	**PX/PF PX**		**PF**	**XR**
ZAMBIA		**Total Exports**			
Tegene, (1990) 1973:1-1985:4	0.31	-0.20*			
Truett and Truett, (1992) 1967-1987	0.774	-0.532			

* denotes statistical significance at the .05 level

Table 4.2   Export Demand Elasticities by Country Total Merchandise Exports Minus Various Categories

COUNTRY	Category				
Author, (Year) Period	YF	PX/PF	PX	PF	XR
AUSTRALIA		Non-Energy			
Bosworth, (1993) 1970-1990	0.20	-0.66*			
AUSTRIA		Non-Energy			
Bosworth, (1993) 1970-1990	0.92*	-0.63			
BELGIUM		Non-Energy			
Bosworth, (1993) 1970-1990	1.39*	-1.48*			
CANADA		Non-Energy			
Bosworth, (1993) 1970-1990	0.23	-0.96*			

* denotes statistical significance at the .05 level

Table 4.2 (Continued)

COUNTRY	Category				
Author, (Year) Period	YF	PX/PF	PX	PF	XR
DENMARK		Non-Energy			
Bosworth, (1993) 1970-1990	0.68*	-1.04*			
FRANCE		Non-Energy			
Bosworth, (1993) 1970-1990	1.11*	-1.18*			
GERMANY		Non-Energy			
Bosworth, (1993) 1970-1990	0.67*	-0.29			
GREECE		Non-Fuel			
Halikias, (1995) 1961-1992	1.55*		-1.12*	1.52*	

* denotes statistical significance at the .05 level

Table 4.2 (Continued)

COUNTRY	Category				
Author, (Year) Period	YF	PX/PF	PX	PF	XR
ITALY		Non-Energy			
Bosworth, (1993) 1970-1990	0.70*	-0.76*			
JAPAN		Non-Energy			
Bosworth, (1993) 1970-1990	1.57*	-0.51*			
NETHERLANDS		Non-Energy			
Bosworth, (1993) 1970-1990	0.91*	-0.33			
SINGAPORE		Non-Oil			
Abeysinghe and Tan, (1998) 1975-1992	1.95*				-1.66*

* denotes statistical significance at the .05 level

Table 4.2 (Continued)

COUNTRY	Category				
Author, (Year) Period	YF	PX/PF	PX	PF	XR
SPAIN Non-Energy					
Buisan and Gordo, (1994) 1964-1992	1.67*	-1.19*			
SWEDEN Non-Energy					
Bosworth, (1993) 1970-1990	0.46*	-0.92*			
UNITED KINGDOM Non-Energy					
Bosworth, (1993) 1970-1990	0.27*	-0.59*			
UNITED STATES Non-Agricultural					
Clark, (1977) 1960:1-1973:2	1.03*	-0.906*			
Feldman, (1984) 1971:3-1980:2	1.88*	-1.33*			
Helkie and Hooper, (1987) 1969:1-1984:4	2.19*	-0.83*			

* denotes statistical significance at the .05 level

Table 4.2 (Continued)

COUNTRY	Category				
Author, (Year) **Period**	YF	PX/PF	PX	PF	XR
UNITED STATES (Continued)					
	Non-Agricultural (Continued)				
Krugman and Baldwin, (1987) 1977:2-1986:4	2.92*				-1.33*
Helkie and Hooper, (1988) 1969:1-1984:4	2.19*	-0.83*			
Hooper and Mann, (1989) 1969:1-1984:4	1.91*	-0.95*			
Blecker, (1992) 1977:1-1990:3	1.67*	-0.67*			
Hickok and Hung, (1992) 1967:1-1988:4	1.90*	-0.45*			

* denotes statistical significance at the .05 level

**Table 4.3   Export Demand Elasticities by Country
Broad Commodity Categories for Exports**

COUNTRY	Category				
Author, (Year) Period	YF	PX/PF	PX	PF	XR
AUSTRALIA					
Manufacturing					
Bosworth, (1993) 1970-1990	0.46	-0.40			
Travel Services					
Moshirian, (1993) 1964-1986	0.57	-0.88*			
AUSTRIA					
Manufacturing					
Deppler and Ripley, (1978) 1964:1-1976:1	1.08*	-1.04*			
Krugman, (1989) 1971-1986	3.05*	-0.60			
Bosworth, (1993) 1970-1990	0.85*	-0.99*			
BELGIUM					
Manufacturing					
Krugman, (1989) 1971-1986	1.24*	-0.19*			

* denotes statistical significance at the .05 level

Table 4.3 (Continued)

COUNTRY	Category				
Author, (Year) Period	YF	PX/PF	PX	PF	XR
BELGIUM (Continued)					
Manufacturing (Continued)					
Bosworth, (1993) 1970-1990	1.40*	-0.55*			
BRAZIL					
Agricultural					
Zini, (1988) 1970:1-1986:3	0.305		-0.346*	0.195	
Industrial					
Lemgruber, (1976) 1965-1974	2.53*	-0.68			
Braga and Markwald, (1983) 1959-1981	2.59*	-2.82			
Pinto, (1983) 1954-1975	2.19*	-1.12			
Zini, (1988) 1970:1-1986:3	1.70*		-0.162	0.242	
Manufacturing					
Rios, (1987) 1964-1984	2.2435*	-1.5918*			

* denotes statistical significance at the .05 level

Table 4.3 (Continued)

COUNTRY	Category				
Author, (Year) Period	YF	PX/PF	PX	PF	XR

BRAZIL (Continued)

Mineral

Zini, (1988) 1970:1-1986:3	0.668*		-0.018	0.228*	

CANADA

Travel Services

Moshirian, (1993) 1964-1986	3.1*	-1.3*			

DENMARK

Manufacturing

Deppler and Ripley, (1978) 1967:1-1976:1	1.08*	-0.93*			
Bosworth, (1993) 1970-1990	0.96*	-1.06*			

FINLAND

Travel Services

Moshirian, (1993) 1964-1986	2.5*	-1.1*			

* denotes statistical significance at the .05 level

Table 4.3 (Continued)

COUNTRY	Category				
Author, (Year) Period	YF	PX/PF	PX	PF	XR
FRANCE					
	Manufacturing				
Deppler and Ripley, (1978) 1964:1-1976:1	0.70*	-1.97*			
Bosworth, (1993) 1970-1990	1.30*	-1.04*			
	Travel Services				
Moshirian, (1993) 1970-1986	2.1*	-2.5*			
GERMANY					
	Machinery and Transport				
Bushe, et al., (1986) 1953-1981	2.25*	-0.61*			
	Manufacturing				
Deppler and Ripley, (1978) 1964:1-1976:1	1.11*	-0.66*			
Akhtar and Hilton, (1984) 1974-1981	2.21*	-2.38*			
Krugman, (1989) 1971-1986	2.15*	-0.55			

* denotes statistical significance at the .05 level

Table 4.3 (Continued)

COUNTRY	Category				
Author, (Year) Period	YF	PX/PF	PX	PF	XR

GERMANY (Continued)

Manufacturing (Continued)

Funke and Holly, (1992) 1961:1-1987:4	0.68*	-0.16			
Bosworth, (1993) 1970-1990	1.06*	-0.41*			

Mechanical Engineering

Funke and Holly, (1992) 1970:1-1987:4	0.47*	-0.11			

Motor Vehicles

Funke and Holly, (1992) 1970:1-1987:4	0.68*	-0.09			

Travel Services

Moshirian, (1993) 1964-1986	0.14	-1.0*			

GREECE

Agricultural

Halikias, (1988) 1961-1985	1.4*	-0.8*			

* denotes statistical significance at the .05 level

Table 4.3 (Continued)

COUNTRY	Category				
Author, (Year) Period	YF	PX/PF	PX	PF	XR
GREECE (Continued)					
	Agricultural (Continued)				
Halikias, (1995) 1961-1992	0.64*		-1.07*	1.54*	
	Manufacturing				
Halikias, (1988) 1961-1985	1.3*	-1.6*			
Balassa, et al., (1989) 1960-1978	4.07*	-3.43*			
Halikias, (1995) 1961-1992	1.81*		-1.25*	1.56*	
	Raw Materials				
Halikias, (1995) 1961-1992	1.03*		-0.79*	0.52*	
	Travel Services				
Moshirian, (1993) 1964-1986	2.7*	-1.1*			

* denotes statistical significance at the .05 level

Table 4.3 (Continued)

COUNTRY	Category				
Author, (Year) Period	YF	PX/PF	PX	PF	XR
HONG KONG					
	Manufacturing				
Riedel, (1988) 1972:1-1984:4	4.0*	-0.70*			
Muscatilli, et al., (1995) 1966-1987	0.83*	-1.28*			
INDIA					
	Chemicals				
Nguyen and Bhuyan, (1977) 1957-1969	2.938*	-0.708*			
	Crude Materials				
Nguyen and Bhuyan, (1977) 1957-1969	1.453*	-0.441*			
	Electric Machines				
Lucas, (1988) 1964-1980	1.172*	-1.376*			
	Food				
Nguyen and Bhuyan, (1977) 1957-1969	0.946*	-0.402*			

* denotes statistical significance at the .05 level

Table 4.3 (Continued)

COUNTRY	Category				
Author, (Year) Period	YF	PX/PF	PX	PF	XR

INDIA (Continued)

Machinery and Transport

Nguyen and Bhuyan, (1977) 1957-1969	8.360*	-0.846*			

Manufacturing

Nguyen and Bhuyan, (1977) 1957-1969	1.641*	-0.644*			

Metal

Lucas, (1988) 1964-1980	1.782*	-0.684*			

Motor Vehicles

Lucas, (1988) 1964-1980	1.507*	-2.527*			

Non Electric Machines

Lucas, (1988) 1964-1980	1.851*	-0.979*			

Non Metal Products

Lucas, (1988) 1964-1980	2.082*	-1.037			

* denotes statistical significance at the .05 level

Table 4.3 (Continued)

COUNTRY	Category				
Author, (Year) Period	YF	PX/PF	PX	PF	XR
ISRAEL					
	Industrial				
Zilberfarb, (1980) 1955-1975	1.13*	-0.62*			
ITALY					
	Manufacturing				
Orsi, (1982) 1967:1-1979:4	1.25*	-1.26*			
Krugman, (1989) 1971-1986	2.41*	-0.23			
Bosworth, (1993) 1970-1990	0.51*	-0.63*			
	Travel Services				
Moshirian, (1993) 1964-1986	0.85*	-1.6*			
JAPAN					
	Machinery and Transport				
Bushe, et al., (1986) 1953-1981	1.53*	-0.97*			

* denotes statistical significance at the .05 level

Table 4.3 (Continued)

COUNTRY	Category				
Author, (Year) Period	YF	PX/PF	PX	PF	XR

JAPAN (Continued)

Manufacturing

Deppler and Ripley, (1978) 1964:1-1976:1	1.45*	-1.73*			
Lawrence, (1987) 1970-1985	1.39*				-0.75*
Bosworth, (1993) 1970-1990	1.45*	-0.57*			

KOREA

Manufacturing

Muscatelli, et al., (1995) 1966-1987	2.45*	-1.65*			

NETHERLANDS

Manufacturing

Deppler and Ripley, (1978) 1964:1-1976:1	0.65*	-1.87*			
Krugman, (1989) 1971-1986	3.86*	-0.76*			
Bosworth, (1993) 1970-1990	1.39*	-0.76*			

* denotes statistical significance at the .05 level

Table 4.3 (Continued)

COUNTRY	Category				
Author, (Year) Period	YF	PX/PF	PX	PF	XR
NEW ZEALAND					
		Manufacturing			
Joumard and Reisen, (1992) 1980:1-1990:3	1.02*				-0.48*
NORWAY					
		Manufacturing			
Deppler and Ripley, (1978) 1964:1-1976:1	0.75*	-2.89*			
PAKISTAN					
		Crude Materials			
Nguyen and Bhuyan, (1977) 1954-1968	0.767*	-0.508*			
		Manufacturing			
Nguyen and Bhuyan, (1977) 1954-1968	3.266*	-1.334*			
SINGAPORE					
		Services			
Abeysinghe and Tan, (1998) 1975-1992	2.64*				-1.67*

* denotes statistical significance at the .05 level

Table 4.3 (Continued)

COUNTRY	Category				
Author, (Year) **Period**	**YF**	**PX/PF**	**PX**	**PF**	**XR**

SPAIN

Travel Services

Moshirian, (1993) 1972-1986	2.1*	-1.9*

SWEDEN

Manufacturing

Deppler and Ripley, (1978) 1964:1-1976:1	1.14*	-1.83*

Bosworth, (1993) 1970-1990	0.74*	-1.04*

Travel Services

Moshirian, (1993) 1964-1986	3.1*	-1.2*

SWITZERLAND

Manufacturing

Deppler and Ripley, (1978) 1964:1-1976:1	0.82*	-1.57*

Travel Services

Moshirian, (1993) 1964-1986	2.1*	-0.77*

* denotes statistical significance at the .05 level

Table 4.3 (Continued)

COUNTRY	Category				
Author, (Year) Period	YF	PX/PF	PX	PF	XR
TAIWAN		Manufacturing			
Musratelli, et al., (1995) 1966-1987	1.39*	-0.16			
THAILAND		Manufacturing			
Muscatelli, et al., (1995) 1966-1987	0.82*	-1.36*			
UNITED KINGDOM		Manufacturing			
Deppler and Ripley, (1978) 1964:1-1976:1	0.90*	-0.54			
Brooks, (1981) 1964:1-1977:3	0.572*	-0.6867*			
Anderton and Dunnett, (1987) 1966:1-1986:1	0.61*	-0.61*			
Krugman, (1989) 1971-1986	1.30*	-0.54*			
Holly and Wade, (1991) 1965:2-1982:4	0.704*	-0.945*			

* denotes statistical significance at the .05 level

Table 4.3 (Continued)

COUNTRY	Category				
Author, (Year) Period	YF	PX/PF	PX	PF	XR
UNITED KINGDOM (Continued)					
	Manufacturing (Continued)				
Anderton, et al., (1992) 1966:2-1987:1	0.67*	-0.51*			
Bosworth, (1993) 1970-1990	0.12	-0.71*			
	Travel Services				
Moshirian, (1993) 1964-1986	2.5*	-0.99*			
UNITED STATES					
	Agricultural				
Clark, (1977) 1959:3-1972:4	0.25*	-0.38*			
Helkie and Hooper, (1988) 1969:1-1984:4	1.15*	-0.93*			
	Farm Commodities				
Batten and Belongia, (1986) 1971:1-1985:2	1.325*	-0.298*			-0.721*
Belongia, (1986) 1973:1-1985:1	0.819*	-0.643*			-0.878*

* denotes statistical significance at the .05 level

Table 4.3 (Continued)

COUNTRY	Category				
Author, (Year) Period	YF	PX/PF	PX	PF	XR

UNITED STATES (Continued)

Finished Manufacturing

Sawyer and Sprinkle, (1997) 1958:1-1987:4	0.9497*		-1.1302*	1.0636*	-0.9275*

Machinery and Transport

Buhse, et al., (1986) 1953-1981	1.48*	-1.27*			

Manufacturing

Lawrence, (1978) 1962:2-1977:2	1.43*	-1.85*			
Akhtar and Hilton, (1984) 1974-1981	1.00*	-1.37*			
Kim, (1992) 1975:1-1989:4	0.81*	-0.47*			
Bosworth, (1993) 1970-1990	0.40	-1.12*			

Non-Agricultural and Computer

Lawrence, (1990) 1976:1-1990:1	1.60*	-0.32*			

* denotes statistical significance at the .05 level

Table 4.3 (Continued)

COUNTRY	Category				
Author, (Year) Period	**YF**	**PX/PF**	**PX**	**PF**	**XR**

UNITED STATES (Continued)

		Travel Services			
Moshirian, (1993) 1964-1986	2.2*	-0.51			

* denotes statistical significance at the .05 level

5 Summary and Conclusions

The results presented in Chapters 3 and 4 suggest several things about the demand for imports and exports in the world economy. Even with this large body of literature, there are areas where the state of knowledge is somewhat inadequate. First our knowledge of the responsiveness of imports and exports to changes in the exchange rate is small at best. Given the importance of the subject, there is a paucity of information both for imports and exports. Second, there appears to be non-trivial differences in the responsiveness of trade flows to changes in domestic versus foreign prices. This is especially the case with respect to imports and the price-ratio specification may often mask as much information as it is giving. Third, the use of specifications with lags is declining in the literature. This is unfortunate as with the exception of income, the response of imports and exports to changes in relative prices and/or exchange rates is hardly instantaneous. In part, this has probably been a consequence of the preoccupation of researchers with using the new econometric techniques. Initially these techniques were not amenable for use with specifications using any type of significant lag structure.

With regards to the newer econometric techniques, a problem may have arisen in this literature with respect to cointegration. There may be a tendency to view proof of cointegration as also being a specification test. This may not always be the case. Finding that the dependent and independent variables are cointegrated does not mean that a relatively simple specification is necessarily correctly specified.

Some researchers use both tests for cointergation and specification tests. This may lead researchers back to issues involving the lag structures of some of the various price variables. In this case, estimated elasticities may have the advantage of being both more technically correct and more useful.

Finally, the estimates presented in the previous chapters are helpful but also difficult to interpret. The results of various strudies in general are sensitive to two factors. First, various specifications may lead to somewhat different estimated coefficients. Second, differences in the time series utilized may lead to somewhat different results. In this regard, a conventional wisdom has developed that at least on the import side, these elasticities are changing over time. The data presented in the tables is useful for obtaining a general idea of the elasticities of import and exports demand for various countries. More specific assumptions about changes in these elasticities or the short-run dynamics of these relationships is tentative at best.

Bibliography

Abeysinghe, T. and Tan, L. Y., "Exchange Rate Appreciation and Export Competitiveness: The Case of Singapore", *Applied Economics*, January 1998, 30(1), pp. 51-55.

Agarwal, Mangat Ram, "Devaluation, Determinants of International Trade Flows and Payments Imbalances", *Indian Economic Journal*, January-March 1984, 31(3), pp. 24-33.

Ajayi, S. Ibi, "Econometric Analysis of Import Demand Function for Nigeria", *Nigerian Journal of Economic and Social Studies*, 1985, 17, pp. 169-182.

Akhtar, M. A., "Manufacturing Import Functions for the United Kingdom, West Germany, and France", *Economia Internazionale*, May-August 1979, 32(2), pp. 181-199.

Akhtar, M. A., "Income and Price Elasticities of Imports in Industrial Countries", *Business Economics*, September 1980, 15(4), pp. 69-75.

Akhtar, M. A., "Manufacturing Import Functions for Canada, Japan, and the United States", *Hitotsubashi Journal of Economics*, June 1981, 22(1), pp. 61-71.

Akhtar, M. A., "Income and Price Elasticities of Non-Oil Imports for Six Industrial Countries", *The Manchester School of Social and Economic Studies*, December 1981, 49(4), pp. 334-347.

Akhtar, M. A. and R. Spence Hilton, "Effects of Exchange-Rate Uncertainty on German and U.S. Trade", *Federal Reserve Bank of New York Quarterly Review*, Spring 1984, 9(1), pp. 7-16.

Amano, Robert A. and Tony S. Wirjanto, "Adjustment Costs and Import Demand Behavior: Evidence from Canada and the United States", *Journal of International Money and Finance*, June 1997, 16(3), pp. 461-476.

Andersen, P. S., "The 45-Rule Revisited", *Applied Economics*, October 1993, 25(10), pp. 1279-1284.

Anderton, B., B. Pesaran, and S. Wren-Lewis, "Imports, Output, and the Demand for Manufactures", *Oxford Economic Papers*, April 1992, 44(2), pp. 175-186.

Anderton, R. and M. Desai, "Modelling Manufacturing Imports", *National Institute Economic Review*, February 1988, (123), pp. 80-86.

Anderton, R. and A. Dunnett, "Modelling the Behavior of Export Volumes of Manufactures: An Evaluation of the Performance of Different Measures of International Competitiveness", *National Institute Economic Review*, August 1987, (121), pp. 46-52.

Arize, Augustine C., "The Elasticities and Structural Stability of Import Demand Function for Nigeria (1960-1977)", *Social and Economic Studies*, June 1987, 36(2), pp. 171-186.

Arize, Augustine C., "The Supply and Demand for Imports and Exports in A Simultaneous Model", *Applied Economics*, September 1987, 19(9), pp. 1233-1247.

Arize, Augustine C., "Modeling Export Price and Quantities in Selected Developing Countries", *Atlantic Economic Journal*, March 1988, 16(1), pp. 19-24.

Arize, Augustine C., "The Demand and Supply for Exports in Nigeria in A Simultaneous Model", *Indian Economic Journal*, April-June 1988, 35(4), pp. 33-43.

Arize, Augustine C., "An Econometric Investigation of Export Behavior in Seven Asian Developing Countries", *Applied Economics*, July 1990, 22(7), pp. 891-904.

Arize, Augustine C., "Specification Tests of the Aggregate Import Demand Model in Developing Countries", *International Economic Journal*, Spring 1991, 5(1), pp. 79-89.

Arize, Augustine C., "The Effects of Exchange-Rate Volatility on U.S. Exports: An Empirical Investigation", *Southern Economic Journal*, July 1995, 62(1), pp. 34-43.

Arize, Augustine C., "A Reexamination of the Demand for U.K. Exports: Evidence from An Error Correction Model", *International Trade Journal*, Winter 1996, 10(4), pp. 501-524.

Arize, Augustine C. and Rasoul Afifi, "An Econometric Examination of Import Demand Function in Thirty Developing Countries", *Journal of Post Keynesian Economics*, Summer 1987, 9(4), pp. 604-616.

Arize, Augustine C. and J. B. Spalding, "A Statistical Demand Function for Imports in South Korea", *Journal of Economic Development*, June 1991, 16(1), pp. 147-164.

Arize, Augustine C. and Jan Walker, "A Reexamination of Japan's Aggregate Import Demand Function: An Application of the Engle and Granger Two-Step Procedure", *International Economic Journal*, Summer 1992, 6(2), pp. 41-55.

Asseery, A. and D. A. Peel, "Estimates of A Traditional Aggregate Import Demand Model for Five Countries", *Economics Letters*, April 1991, 35(4), pp. 435-439.

Asseery, A. and D. A. Peel, "The Effects of Exchange Rate Volatility on Exports: Some New Estimates", *Economics Letters*, October 1991, 37(2), pp. 173-177.

Asseery, A. and N. Perdikis, "Estimating the Aggregate Import Demand Functions of the G.C.C.'s Member States for the Period 1970-1985", *Middle East Business and Economic Review*, July 1990, 2(2), pp. 1-8.

Asseery, A. A. and N. Perdikis, "An Empirical Investigation into the Determinants of Cyprus Aggregate Import and Export Functions", *Middle East Business and Economic Review*, July 1991, 3(2), pp. 23-26.

Asseery, A. A. and N. Perdikis, "The Functional Form of the Aggregate Import Demand Function: The Case of the GCC Countries", *Middle East Business and Economic Review*, January 1993, 5(1), pp. 34-38.

Athukorala, Premachandra and Jaynant Menon, "Modeling Manufactured Imports: Methodological Issues with Evidence From Australia", *Journal of Policy Modeling*, December 1995, 17(6), pp. 667-675.

Athukorala, Premachandra and James Riedel, "The Small Country Assumption: A Reassessment with Evidence from Korea", *Weltwirtschaftliches Archiv*, 1991, 127(1), pp. 138-151.

Aurikko, Esko, "A Dynamic Disaggregated Model of Finnish Imports of Goods", *Empirical Economics*, 1985, 10(2), pp. 103-120.

Aurikko, Esko, "Testing Disequilibrium Adjustment Models for Finnish Exports of Goods", *Oxford Bulletin of Economics and Statistics*, February 1985, 47(1), pp. 33-50.

Aurikko, Esko, "Testing the Functional Form of Finnish Aggregate Imports", *Economics Letters*, 1985, 18, pp. 223-228.

Babula, Ronald A., "An Armington Model of U.S. Cotton Exports", *Journal of Agricultural Economics Research*, Fall 1987, 39(4), pp. 12-22.

Bahmani-Oskooee, Moshen, "On the Effect of Effective Exchange Rates on Trade Flows", *Indian Journal of Economics,* July 1984, 65, pp. 57-67.

Bahmani-Oskooee, Moshen, "Determinants of International Trade Flows - The Case of Developing Countries", *Journal of Development Economics*, January-February 1986, 20(1), pp. 107-123.

Bahmani-Oskooee, Moshen, "On the Effects of U.S. Federal Deficits on Its Trade Flows", *Journal of Post Keynesian Economics*, Fall 1991, 14(1), pp. 72-82.

Bahmani-Oskooee, Moshen and Farhang Niroomand, "Long-Run Price Elasticities and the Marshall-Lerner Condition", *Economics Letters*, 1998, 61(1), pp. 101-109.

Bahmani-Oskooee, Mohsen and H. J. Rhee, "Are Imports and Exports of Korea Cointegrated?", *International Economic Journal*, Spring 1997, 11(1), pp. 109-114.

Bahmani-Oskooee, Mohsen and H. J. Rhee, "Structural Change in Import Demand Behavior, the Korean Experience", *Journal of Policy Modeling*, April 1997, 19(2), pp. 187-193.

Bailey, Martin J., George S. Tavlas, and Michael Ulan, "Exchange-Rate Variability and Trade Performance: Evidence for the Big Seven Industrial Countries", *Weltwirtschaftliches Archiv*, 1986, 122(3), pp. 466-477.

Bailey, Martin J., George S. Tavlas, and Michael Ulan, "The Impact of Exchange-Rate Volatility on Export Growth: Some Theoretical Considerations and Empirical Results", *Journal of Policy Modeling*, Spring 1987, 9(1), pp. 225-243.

Balassa, Bela, Evangelos Voloudakis, Panagiotis Flyaktos, and Suk T. Suh, "The Determinants of Export Supply and Export Demand in Two Developing Countries: Greece and Korea", *International Economic Journal*, Spring 1989, 3(1), pp. 1-16.

Baldwin, Richard, "Hysteresis in Import Prices: The Beachhead Effect", *American Economic Review*, September 1988, 78(4), pp. 773-785.

Batten, Dallas S. and Michael T. Belongia, "Monetary Policy, Real Exchange Rates, and U.S. Agricultural Exports", *American Journal of Agricultural Economics*, May 1986, 68(2), pp. 422-427.

Bautista, Romeo M., "Effects of Major Currency Realignment on Philippine Merchandise Trade", *Review of Economics and Statistics*, May 1977, 59(2), pp. 152-160.

Bautista, Romeo M., "Import Demand in A Small Country with Trade Restrictions", *Oxford Economic Papers*, July 1978, 30(2), pp. 199-216.

Bautista, Romeo M., "Import Demand for Capital Equipment in the Philippines", *Weltwirtschaftliches Archiv*, 1980, 116(3), pp. 560-573.

Beenstock, M. and P. Minford, "A Quarterly Econometric Model of Trade and Prices 1955-72", in Michael Parkin and George Zis, eds, *Inflation in Open Economies*, Manchester: Manchester University Press, 1976, pp. 85-125.

Beenstock, Michael and Peter Warburton, "UK Imports and the International Trading Order", *Weltwirtschaftliches Archiv*, 1982, 118(4), pp. 707-725.

Belongia, Michael. T., "Estimating Exchange Rate Effects on Exports: A Cautionary Note", *Federal Reserve Bank of St. Louis Economic Review*, January 1986, 68(1), pp. 5-15.

Bergstrand, Jeffrey H., "The U.S. Trade Deficit: A Perspective from Selected Bilateral Trade Models", *New England Economic Review*, May-June 1987, pp. 19-31.

Bewley, Ronald and David Orden, "Alternative Methods for Estimating Long-Run Responses with Applications to Australian Import Demand", *Econometric Reviews*, 1994, 13(2), pp. 179-204.

Bini-Smaghi L., "Exchange Rate Variability and Trade: Why Is It So Difficult to Find Any Empirical Relationship?", *Applied Economics*, May 1991, 23(5), pp. 927-935.

Biswas, Basudeb and Rati Ram, "Demand Function for India's Foodgrain Imports: Some Elasticity Estimates", *Indian Economic Journal*, April-June 1980, 27(4), pp. 12-19.

Blecker, Robert A., "Structural Roots of U.S. Trade Problems: Income Elasticities, Secular Trends, and Hysteresis", *Journal of Post Keynesian Economics*, Spring 1992, 14(3), pp. 321-346.

Bosworth, Barry P., *Saving and Investment in a Global Economy*, Washington, D.C.: Brookings Institution, 1993.

Boylan, T. A. and M. P. Cuddy, "Elasticities of Import Demand and Economic Development: The Irish Experience", *Journal of Development Economics*, August 1987, 26(2), pp. 301-309.

Boylan, T. A.,. M. P. Cuddy, and I. O'Muircheartaigh, "The Irish Import Demand Equation: The Optimal Functional Form", *Economic and Social Review*, January 1979, 10(12), pp. 147-156.

Boylan, T. A., M. P. Cuddy, and I. O'Muercheartaigh, "The Functional Form of the Aggregate Import Demand Function: A Comparison of Three European Economies", *Journal of International Economics*, November 1980, 10(4), pp. 561-566.

Boylan, T. A., M. P. Cuddy, and I. O'Muircheartaigh, "Import Demand Equations: An Application of A Generalized Box-Cox Methodology", *International Statistical Review*, 1981, 50, pp. 103-112.

Braga, Helson and Ricardo Markwald, "Funcoes de oferta e de demanda das exportacoes de manufaturados no Brasil", *Pesquisa e Planejamento Economico*, December 1983, 31(3), pp. 707-744.

Brooks, S., "Systematic Econometric Comparisons: Exports of Manufactured Goods", *National Institute Economic Review*, August 1981, 97, pp. 67-80.

Buisan, Ana and Esther Gordo, "Funciones De Importacion Y Exportacion De La Economia Espanola", *Investigaciones Economicas*, January 1994, 18(1), pp. 165-192.

Bushe, Dennis M, Irving B. Kravis, and Robert E. Lipsey, "Prices, Activity, and Machinery Exports: An Analysis Based on New Price Data", *Review of Economics and Statistics*, May 1986, 68(2), pp. 248-255.

Caporole, Tony and Khosrow Doroodian, "Exchange Rate Variability and the Flow of International Trade", *Economics Letters*, September 1994, 46(1), pp. 49-54.

Carone, G., "Modeling the U.S. Demand for Imports through Cointegration and Error Correction", *Journal of Policy Modeling*, February 1996, 18(1), pp. 1-48.

Ceglowski, Janet, "On the Structural Stability of Trade Equations: The Case of Japan", *Journal of International Money and Finance*, June 1997, 16(3), pp. 491-512.

Chan, Patrick K. L. and Jim H. Y. Wong, "The Effect of Exchange Rate Variability on Hong Kong's Exports", *Hong Kong Economic Papers*, 1985, (16), pp. 27-39.

Cheng, H. S., "Statistical Estimates of Elasticities and Propensities in International Trade: A Survey", *IMF Staff Papers*, March 1959, 7(1), pp. 107-158.

Chou, W. L. and Y. C. Shih, "Trade, Determinants, and Causality: A Case of Hong Kong's Exports to the United States", *International Economic Journal*, Winter 1988, 2(4), pp. 21-33.

Cima, Lawrence R., "The Excess Supply-Pure Demand Approach to International Commodity Trade: The Case of Japanese Steel Exports to the United States", *Economic Inquiry*, October 1986, 24(4), pp. 645-656.

Citrin, Daniel, "Exchange Rate Changes and Exports of Selected Japanese Industries", *IMF Staff Papers*, September 1985, 32(3), pp. 404-429.

Clarida, Richard H., "Cointegration, Aggregate Consumption, and the Demand for Imports: A Structural Econometric Investigation", *American Economic Review*, March 1994, 84(1), pp. 298-308.

Clark, Don P., "The Effects of the Exchange Rate of the U.S. Dollar on Developing Countries' Import Demand", Working Paper, 1992.

Clark, Peter B., "The Effects of Recent Exchange Rate Changes on the U.S. Trade Balance", in *The Effects of Exchange Rate Adjustments*, Peter B. Clark, Dennis E. Logue, and Richard J. Sweeney, (eds.), Washington, D.C.: U.S. Government Printing Office, 1977, pp. 201-236.

Clavijo, Fernando and Riccardo Faini, "Las Elasticidades Ingreso Ciclicas y Seculares de La Demanda de Importaciones en los Paises in Desarrollo", *El Trimestre Economico* January-March 1990, 57 (225), pp. 89-100.

Cline, William, *United States External Adjustment and the World Economy*, Washington, D.C.: Institute for International Economics, 1989.

Conway, R. G., "An Examination of the 'Schuh Controversy': Is the Demand for U.S. Agricultural Exports Elastic?", *Applied Economics*, July 1987, 19(7), pp. 853-873.

Corker, Robert, "External Adjustment and the Strong Yen: Recent Japanese Experience", *IMF Staff Papers*, June 1989, 36(2), pp. 464-493.

Craig, Sean, "Japanese Bilateral Trade Elasticities, Memorandum", *Division of International Finance*, Federal Reserve Board, Washington, D.C., 1986.

Cuthbertson, K., "The Behaviour of UK Imports of Manufactured Goods", *National Institute Economic Review*, August 1985, (113), pp. 31-38.

de Melo, Jaime, Marcelo Olarreaga, and Wendy Tackas, "Pricing Strategy Under Eroding Monopoly Power: The International Vanilla Market", Paper Prepared for the Conference *Recent Developments in International Trade*, Aix en Provence, June 1995.

Deppler, M. C. and D. M. Ripley, "The World Trade Model: The Merchandise Trade", *IMF Staff Papers*, March 1978, 25(1), pp. 147-206.

Deyak, Timothy A., W. Charles Sawyer, and Richard L. Sprinkle, "An Empirical Examination of the Structural Stability of Disaggregated U.S. Import Demand", *Review of Economics and Statistics*, May 1989, 71(2), pp. 337-341.

Deyak, Timothy A., W. Charles Sawyer, and Richard L. Sprinkle, "The Effects of Exchange Rate Changes on Prices and Quantities in U.S. Foreign Trade", *International Trade Journal*, Fall 1990, 5(1), pp. 77-92.

Deyak, Timothy A., W. Charles Sawyer, and Richard L. Sprinkle, "A Comparison of the Demand for Imports and Exports in Japan and the United States", *Journal of World Trade*, October 1993, 27(5), pp. 63-74.

Deyak, Timothy A., W. Charles Sawyer, and Richard L. Sprinkle, "The Adjustment of Canadian Import Demand to Changes in Income, Prices, and Exchange Rates", *Canadian Journal of Economics*, November 1993, 26(4), pp. 890-900.

Deyak, Timothy A., W. Charles Sawyer, and Richard L. Sprinkle, "Changes in the Price and Income Elasticities of U.S. Import Demand", *Economia Internazionale*, May 1997, 50(2), pp. 161-175.

Di Liberto, Maryann F., "A Test for Structural Change in U.S. Real Trade and Trade Prices: Fixed Exchange Rate Period vs. Flexible Exchange Rate Period", *International Trade Journal*, Summer 1988, 2(4), pp. 337-375.

Dib, Maria de Fatima, "Equacoes para a demanda de importacoes no Brasil - 1960/79", *Revista Brasileira de Economia*, 1981, 35(1), 373-386.

Dixit, Avinash K., "Hysteresis, Import Penetration, and Exchange Rate Pass-Through", *Quarterly Journal of Economics*, May 1989, 104(2), pp. 205-228.

Doroodian, Khosrow, "The Permanent Income Theory of Demand for Imports of Finished Manufactured Goods: The Case of the United States", *Quarterly Journal of Business and Economics*, Winter 1987, 26(1), pp. 78-85.

Doroodian, Khosrow, Rajindar K. Koshal, and Saleh Al-Muhanna, "An Examination of the Traditional Aggregate Import Demand Function for Saudi Arabia", *Applied Economics*, September 1994, 26(9), pp. 909-915.

Dudley, Leonard, "A Non-Linear Model of Import Demand under Price Uncertainty and Adjustment Costs", *Canadian Journal of Economics*, November 1983, 16(4), pp. 625-640.

Dunlevy, James A., "A Test of the Capacity Pressure Hypothesis Within A Simultaneous Equations Model of Export Performance", *Review of Economics and Statistics*, February 1980, 62(1), pp. 131-135.

Dunlevy, James A. and Timothy A. Deyak, "Seasonal, Cyclical and Secular Stability of Canadian Aggregate Demand for Merchandise Imports, 1957-1982", *Applied Economics*, April 1989, 21(4), pp. 449-459.

Erasmus, C. M., "Elasticities and Lag Structures in South African Imports", *Journal for Studies in Economics and Econometrics*, 1978, 3, pp. 27-51.

Faini, Riccardo, Lant Pritchett, and Fernando Clavijo, "Import Demand in Developing Countries", *World Bank Working Paper*, November 1988.

Faini, Riccardo, Lant Pritchett, and Fernando Clavijo, "Import Demand in Developing Countries", in *International Trade Modelling*, M. G. Dagenais and P-A Muet, eds., London: Chipman and Hall, 1992, pp. 279-297.

Faini, Riccardo, Fernando Clavijo, and A. Senhadji-Semlali, "The Fallacy of Composition Argument; Is It Relevant for LDCs Manufactures Exports?", *European Economic Review*, May 1992, 36(4), pp. 865-882.

Feenstra, Robert C., "New Product Varieties and the Measurement of International Prices", *American Economic Review*, March 1994, 84(1), pp. 157-177.

Feldman, R. A., "The Impact of the Recent Strength of the Dollar on the U.S. Merchandise Trade Balance: Some 'First-Round' Effects and Feedbacks from Exchange Rate Induced Changes in U.S.-Relative Inflation", *Jounal of Policy Modeling*, February 1984, 6(1), pp. 29-44.

Fullerton, Thomas M., W. Charles Sawyer, and Richard L. Sprinkle, "Functional Form for the United States-Mexico Trade Equations", *Estudios Economicos*, Enero-Junio 1997, 12(1), pp. 23-35.

Funke, Michael and Sean Holly, "The Determinants of West German Exports of Manufactures: An Integrated Demand and Supply Approach", *Weltwirtschaftliches Archiv*, 1992, 128(3), pp. 498-512.

Gafar, John S., "Devaluation and the Balance of Payments Adjustment in A Developing Economy: An Analysis Relating to Jamaica: 1954-1972", *Applied Economics*, June 1981, 13(6), pp. 151-165.

Gafar, John S., "Devaluation and Its Impact on the Demand for Imports in An Open Economy: the Case of Jamaica", *Indian Economic Journal*, January-March 1984, 31(3), pp. 34-44.

Gafar, John S., "The Determinants of Import Demand in Trinidad and Tobago: 1967-84", *Applied Economics*, March 1988, 20(3), pp. 303-313.

Gafar, John S., "Some Estimates of the Price and Income Elasticities of Import Demand for Three Caribbean Countries", *Applied Economics*, November 1995, 27(11), pp. 1045-1048.

Gandolfo, Giancarlo and Maria Luisa Petit, "The Functional Form of the Aggregate Import Demand Equation: Italy, 1960-1980", *Economics Letters*, 1983, 11, pp. 145-148.

Geraci, V. J. and W. Prewo, "An Empirical Demand and Supply Model of Multilateral Trade", *Review of Economics and Statistics*, August 1982, 64(3), pp. 432-441.

Giovannetti, G., "Aggregate Imports and Expenditure Components in Italy: An Econometric Analysis", *Applied Economics*, July 1989, 21(7), pp. 957-971.

Goldstein, Morris and Mohsin S. Khan, "Large versus Small Price Changes and the Demand for Imports", *IMF Staff Papers*, 1976, 23(1), pp. 200-225.

Goldstein, Morris and Mohsin S. Khan, "The Supply and Demand for Exports: A Simultaneous Approach", *Review of Economics and Statistics*, May 1978, 60(2), pp. 275-286.

Goldstein, Morris and Mohsin S. Khan, "Income and Price Effects in Foreign Trade", in P.B. Kenen and R. W. Jones (eds.), *Handbook of International Economics*, Amsterdam: North Holland, 1985.

Goldstein, Morris, Mohsin S. Khan, and Lawrence H. Officer, "Prices of Tradable and Non-Tradeable Goods in the Demand for Total Imports", *Review of Economics and Statistics*, May 1980, 62(2), pp. 190-199.

Halikias, John G., "The Determination of Greek Exports: A Disaggregated Model, 1961-1985", *Revista Internazionale di Scienze Economiche e Commerciali*, April-May 1988, 35(4-5), pp. 473-486.

Halikias, John G., "A Disaggregated Model of Greek Exports and Export Prices", *Revista Internazionale di Scienze Economiche e Commerciali*, July-August 1995, 42(7), pp. 649-661.

Hamilton, Carl, "Import Elasticities at A Disaggregated Level: The Case of Sweden", *Scandinavian Journal of Economics*, 1980, 82(4), pp. 449-463.

Haniotis, Tassos, "European Community Enlargement: Impact on U.S. Corn and Soybean Exports", *American Journal of Agricultural Economics*, May 1990, 72(2), pp. 289-297.

Haynes, Stephen E., M. M. Hutchison, and R. F. Mikesell, "U.S.-Japanese Bilateral Trade and the Yen-Dollar Exchange Rate: An Empirical Analysis", *Southern Economic Journal*, April 1986, 52(4), pp. 923-932.

Haynes, Stephen E. and Joe A. Stone, "Spurious Tests and Sign Reversals in International Economics", *Southern Economic Journal*, April 1982, 48(4), pp. 868-876.

Haynes, Stephen E. and Joe A. Stone, "Secular and Cyclical Responses of U.S. Trade to Income: An Evaluation of Traditional Models", *Review of Economics and Statistics*, February 1983, 65(1), pp. 87-95.

Haynes, Stephen E. and Joe A. Stone, "Specification of Supply Behavior in International Trade", *Review of Economics and Statistics*, November 1983, 65(4), pp. 626-631.

Haynes, Stephen E. and Joe A. Stone, "Cross-Price Effects in Demand Between Exports and Imports", *Journal of Macroeconomics*, Spring 1984, 6(2), pp. 181-195.

Heien, Dale and Daniel Pick, "The Structure of International Demand for Soybean Products", *Southern Journal of Agricultural Economics*, July 1991, 23(1), pp. 137-146.

Helkie, William L. and Peter Hooper, "The U.S. External Deficit in the 1980s: An Empirical Analysis", *Federal Reserve Board International Finance Discussion Papers No. 304*, Board of Governors of the Federal Reserve System, Washington, D.C., 1987.

Helkie, William L. and Peter Hooper, "An Empirical Analysis of the External Deficit, 1980-1986", in *External Deficits and the Dollar*, R. C. Bryant, Gerald Holtham, and Peter Hooper, (eds.), Washington, D.C.: Brookings, 1988, pp. 10-56.

Hickok, Susan and Juann Hung, "Explaining the Persistence of the U.S. Trade Deficit in the Late 1980s", *Federal Reserve Bank of New York Quarterly Review*, Winter 1991-1992, 16(4), pp. 29-46.

Hitiris, T. and E. Petoussis, "Price and Tariff Effects in A Dynamic Specification of the Demand for Imports", *Applied Economics*, February 1984, 16(2), pp. 15-24.

Holly, Sean and Keith Wade, "UK Exports of Manufactures: The Role of Supply Side Factors", *Scottish Journal of Political Economy*, February 1991, 38(1), pp. 1-18.

Hooper, Peter and Catherine L. Mann, "Exchange Rate Pass-Through in the 1980s: The Case of U.S. Imports of Manufactures", *Brookings Papers on Economic Activity*, 1989(1), pp. 297-337.

Hooper, Peter and Catherine L. Mann, "The U.S. External Deficit: Its Causes and Persistence", in Albert E. Burger (ed.), *U.S. Trade Deficit: Causes, Consequences, and Cures*, Boston: Kluwer, 1989.

Hooper, Peter, and Jamie Marquez, "Exchange Rates, Prices, and External Adjustment in the United States and Japan", *Federal Reserve Board International Finance Discussion Paper No. 456*, Board of Governors Federal Reserve System, Washington, D.C., 1993.

Hossain, M. Akhtar, "Disaggregated Demand Functions for Bangladesh Exports: Some Econometric Results 1974-1985", *Indian Economic Journal*, January-March 1993, 40(3), pp. 76-96.

Humphrey, D. H., "Disaggregated Import Functions for the United Kingdom, West Germany, and France", *Oxford Bulletin of Economics and Statistics*, November 1976, 58(4), pp. 281-298.

Joseph, Mathew, *Exchange Rate Policy: Impact on Exports and Balance of Payments*, New Delhi: Deep and Deep, 1992.

Joumard, Isabelle and Helmut Reisen, "Real Exchange Rate Overshooting and Persistent Trade Effects: The Case of New Zealand", *World Economy*, May 1992, 15(3), pp. 375-388.

Kabir, Rezaul, "Estimating Import and Export Demand Function: The Case of Bangladesh", *Bangladesh Development Studies*, December 1988, 16(4), pp. 115-127.

Kahn, S. B., "Import Penetration and Import Demands in the South African Economy", *South African Journal of Economics*, September 1987, 55(3), pp. 238-248.

Katayama, Sei-Ichi, Kazuhiro Ohtani, and Toshihisa Toyoda, "Estimation of Structural Change in the Import and Export Equations: An International Comparison", *Economics Studies Quarterly*, June 1987, 38(2), pp. 148-158.

Khan, Moshin S., "The Structure and Behavior of Imports in Venezuela", *Review of Economics and Statistics*, May 1975, 58(2), pp. 221-224.

Khan, Mohsin S. and Knud Z. Ross, "Cyclical and Secular Income Elasticities and the Demand for Imports", *Review of Economics and Statistics*, August 1975, 57(2), pp. 357-361.

Khan, Moshin S. and Knud Z. Ross, "The Functional Form of the Aggregate Import Demand Equation", *Journal of International Economics*, May 1977, 7(2), pp. 149-160.

Kim, Ki- Ho, "Parametric Change in the U.S. Trade in Manufactured Goods", *Atlantic Economic Journal*, September 1992, 20(3), pp. 46-56.

King, Alan, "The Functional Form of Import Demand: The Case of UK Motor Vehicle Imports: 1980-90", *Journal of Economic Studies*, 1993, 20(3), pp. 36-50.

Kohli, Ulrich, *Technology, Duality, and Foreign Trade: The GNP Function Approach to Modeling Imports and Exports*, Ann Arbor: University of Michigan Press, 1991.

Koo, Won W., Ihn Ho Uhm, and Joel T. Golz, "Bilateral Trade Relationship Between the United States and Canada: Implications of the Free Trade Agreement", *Contemporary Policy Issues*, October 1991, 9(4), pp. 56-69.

Koshal, Rajindar K., Khosrow Doroodian, and Ashok Chaluvadi, "The Behavior of Demand and Supply of Thai Imports", *Journal of Asian Economics*, Fall 1993, 4(2), pp. 363-375.

Koshal, Rajindar K., V. Shukla, and G. Koirala, "Demand and Supply of Indian Exports: A Simultaneous Equation Approach", *Journal of Asian Economics*, 1992, 3(1), pp. 73-83.

Krinsky, I., "The Small Country Assumption: A Note on Canadian Exports", *Applied Economics*, February 1983, 15(1), pp. 73-79.

Kroner, Kenneth F. and William D. Lastrapes, "The Impact of Exchange Rate Volatility on International Trade: Reduced Form Estimates Using the GARCH-in-Mean Model", *Journal of International Money and Finance*, June 1993, 12(3), pp. 298-318.

Krugman, Paul, "Differences in Income Elasticities and Trends in Real Exchange Rates", *European Economic Review*, May 1989, 33(5), pp. 1031-1046.

Krugman, Paul R. and Richard. E. Baldwin, "The Persistence of the U.S. Trade Deficit", *Brookings Papers on Economic Activity*, 1987, No. 1, pp. 1-55.

Kumar, Ramesh C. and S. Akbar, "The Generalized System of Preferences and Canadian Imports of Manufactured and Semi-manufactured Products from Developing Countries", *Journal of Economic Studies*, 1983, 10(1), pp. 17-30.

Kumar, Ramesh. C. and Ravinder Dhawan, "Exchange Rate Volatility and Pakistan's Exports to the Developed World, 1974-85", *World Development*, September 1991, 19(9), pp. 1225-1240.

Lachler, Ulrich, "The Elasticity of Substitution Between Imported and Domestically Produced Goods in Germany", *Weltwirtschaftliches Archiv*, 1985, 121(1), pp. 74-96.

Lawrence, Robert Z., "An Analysis of the 1977 U.S. Trade Deficit", *Brookings Papers on Economic Activity*, 1978, 1, pp. 159-190.

Lawrence, Robert Z., "Imports in Japan: Closed Markets or Closed Minds?", *Brookings Papers on Economic Activity*, 1987, 2, pp. 517-548.

Lawrence, Robert Z., "U.S. Current Account Adjustment: An Appraisal", *Brookings Papers on Economic Activity*, No. 2, 1990, pp. 343-392.

Lawrence, Robert Z., "How Open is Japan?", in *Trade with Japan*, Paul Krugman, ed., Chicago: University of Chicago Press, 1991, pp. 9-46.

Lawson, C. W. and C. Thanassoulas, "Predicting West German-Comecon-Imports: A Comparative Assessment of Ordinary Least Squares, Autoregressive Moving Average and Ridge Regression Procedures", *Applied Economics*, August 1982, 14(4), pp. 401-419.

Leamer, E. E. and R. M. Stern, *Quantitative International Economics*, Chicago: Aldine, 1970.

Lemgruber, Antonio C., "Balanco de Pagamentos do Brasil: Uma Analise Quantitativa", *Pesquisa e Planejamento Economico*, August 1976, 6(2), pp. 313-352.

Loopesko, Bonnie and Robert A. Johnson, "Realignment of the Yen-Dollar Exchange Rate: Aspects of the Adjustment Process in Japan", in *Misalignment of Exchange Rates: Effects on Trade and Industry*, Richard C. Marston, ed., Chicago: University of Chicago Press, 1988, pp. 105-144.

Lucas, R. E. B., "Demand for India's Manufactured Exports", *Journal of Development Economics*, July 1988, 29(1), pp. 63-75.

Magee, S., "Prices, Income and Foreign Trade", in *International Trade and Finance: Frontiers for Research*, Peter Kenen, ed., Cambridge University Press, 1975, pp. 175-252.

Mah, J. S., "Structural Change in Import Demand Behavior: The Korean Experience", *Journal of Policy Modeling*, April 1993, 15(2), pp. 223-227.

Marquez, Jaime, "Income and Price Elasticities of Foreign Trade Flows: Econometric Estimation and Analysis of the US Trade Deficit", *Federal Reserve Board International Finance Discussion Paper No. 324*, Board of Governors Federal Reserve System, Washington, D.C., 1988.

Marquez, Jaime, "Bilateral Trade Elasticities", *Review of Economics and Statistics*, February 1990, 72(1), pp. 70-77.

Marquez, Jaime, "The Dynamics of Uncertainty or the Uncertainty of Dynamics: Stochastic J-Curves", *Review of Economics and Statistics*, 1991, 73(1), 125-133.

Marquez, Jaime, "Spectral Estimation of Secular and Cyclical Elasticities for Bilateral Trade", *Finnish Economic Papers*, Autumn 1992, 5(2), pp. 91-97.

Marquez, Jaime, "A Century of Trade Elasticities for Canada, Japan and the United States", 1996.

Marquez, Jaime and Caryl McNeilly, "Income and Price Elasticities for Exports of Developing Countries", *Review of Economics and Statistics*, May 1988, 70(2), pp. 306-314.

Mastropasqua, Cristina, "Was There A Structural Change in the Italian Demand for Aggregate Imports? The Evidence from Quarterly Data, 1960-79", *Economic Notes*, 1982, (1), pp. 65-74.

Medhora, Rohinton, "The Effect of Exchange Rate Variability on Trade: The Case of the West African Monetary Union's Imports", *World Development*, February 1990, 18(2), pp. 313-324.

Meller, P. and M. Cabezas, "Estimacion de las Elasticidades Ingreso y Precio de las Importaciones Chilenas 1974-1987", *Coleccion Estudios CIEPLAN*, June 1989, 26, pp. 127-170.

Melo Oscar and Michael G. Vogt, "Determinants of the Demand for Imports for Venezuela", *Journal of Development Economics*, April 1984, 14(3), pp. 351-358.

Menon, Jayant, "Price and Activity Effects in International Trade: Cointegration, Aggregation and Prices", *Hitotsubashi Journal of Economics*, June 1995, 36(1), pp. 47-60.

Moffett, Michael H., "The J-Curve Revisited,: An Empirical Examination for the United States", *Journal of International Money and Finance*, September 1989, 8(3), pp. 427-444.

Moller, Herbert and Han J. Jarchow, "Demand and Supply Functions for West German Exports", *Jahrbucher fur Nationalokonomie und Statistik*, November 1990, 207(6), pp. 529-538.

Moreno, Ramon, "Exchange Rates and Trade Adjustment in Taiwan and South Korea", *Federal Reserve Bank of San Francisco Economic Review*, Spring 1989, pp. 30-48.

Moreno, Ramon, "Explaining the U.S. Export Boom", *Federal Reserve Bank of San Francisco Economic Review*, Winter 1991, pp. 39-52.

Morgan, A. D., "Tariff Reduction and UK Imports of Manufactures: 1955-71", *National Institute Economic Review*, May 1975, pp. 38-54.

Moshirian, F., "Determinants of International Trade Flows in Services", *Economic Record*, September 1993, 69(206), pp. 239-252.

Murray, Tracy and Peter J. Ginman, "An Empirical Examination of the Traditional Aggregate Import Demand Model", *Review of Economics and Statistics*, February 1976, 58(1), pp. 75-80.

Muscatelli, V. A., A. A. Stevenson, and C. Montagna, "Modeling Aggregate Manufactured Exports for Some Asian Newly Industrialized Economies", *Review of Economics and Statistics*, February 1995, 77(1), pp. 147-155.

Mutti, John H., "The Specification of Demand Equations for Imports and Domestic Substitutes", *Southern Economic Journal*, July 1977, 44(1), pp. 68-73.

Noland, Marcus, "Japanese Trade Elasticities and the J-Curve", *Review of Economics and Statistics*, February 1989, 71(1), pp. 175-179.

Nguyen, D. T. and A. R. Bhuyan, "Elasticities of Export and Import Demand in Some South Asian Countries: Some Estimates", *Bangladesh Development Studies*, April 1977, 5(2), pp. 133-152.

Nyatepe, Coo and A. Akorlie, "Dutch Disease, Government Policy and Import Demand in Nigeria", *Applied Economics*, April 1994, 26(4), pp. 327-336.

O'Neill, Heather M. and William Ross, "Exchange Rate and Income Effects on South Korean Exports: The U.S. Case", *Journal of Economic Development*, December 1991, 16(2), pp. 87-111.

Ohtani, Kazuhiro, Sumio Kakimoto, and Kenzo Abe, "A Gradual Switching Regression Model with a Flexible Transition Path", *Economics Letters*, January 1990, 32(1), pp. 43-48.

Orcutt, G. H., "Measurement of Price Elasticities in International Trade", *Review of Economics and Statistics*, May 1950, 32(2), pp. 117-132.

Orsi, R., "A Simultaneous Disequilibrium Model for Italian Export Goods", *Empirical Economics*, 1982, 7(3/4), pp. 139-154.

Paramosathy, Silvapulla and Prue Phillips, "Australian Import Demand Analysis", in *ASEAN-Australia Trade in Manufactures*, David Lim, ed., Melbourne: Longman-Cheshire, 1985, pp. 108-131.

Parthama, Ida-Bagus P.and Jeffrey R. Vincent, "United States Demand for Indonesian Plywood", *Bulletin of Indonesian Economic Studies*, April 1992, 28(1), pp. 101-112.

Petri, Peter A., "Market Structure, Comparative Advantage, and Japanese Trade under the Strong Yen", in *Trade with Japan*, Paul Krugman, ed., Chicago: University of Chicago Press, 1991, pp. 51-82.

Petoussis, Emmanuel., "The Aggregate Import Function Within A General Equilibrium Context", *Greek Economic Review*, December 1981, 3(3), pp. 310-324.

Petoussis, Emmanuel, "The Aggregate Import Equation: Price Homogeneity and Monetary Effects", *Empirical Economics*, 1985, 10(2), pp. 91-101.

Phaup, E. D., "The Demand for Imports: Estimates of Bilateral Trade Flows", *Journal of Macroeconomics*, Winter 1981, 3(1), pp. 97-115.

Pinto, Mauricio B., "Politica Cambial, Politica Salarial e o Ptentcial das Exportacoes de Manufaturados do Brasil no Perfodo 1954-1974", *Revista Brasileira de Econometria*, November 1983, pp. 87-104.

Pradhan, H. K., "Exchange Rate Variability of the Rupee and India's Exports", *Margin*, July-September 1988, 20(4), pp. 28-47.

Quarcoo, Philip K., "A Study of Ghana's Trade Performance", in *Trade and Development in Sub-Saharan Africa*, Jonathan H. Frimpong-Anash, S. M. Ravi Kanbur, and Peter Svedberg, eds., New York: Manchester University Press, 1991, pp. 314-357.

Riedel, James, "The Demand for LDC Exports of Manufactures: Estimates from Hong Kong", *Economic Journal*, March 1988, 98(389), pp. 138-148.

Rios, S. M. C. P., "Exportacoes Brasileiras de Productos Manufaturados: Uma Avaliacao Econometrica para o Periodo 1964/84", *Pesquisa Planejamento Economico*, August 1987, 26(1), pp. 299-332.

Rojas R., Patricio and Paolo Assael M., "Un Analisis Econometrico de la Demanda por Importaciones Desagregadas en Chile: 1960-1992", *Cuadernos de Economia*, August 1994, 31(93), pp. 251-301.

Salas, Javier, "Estimation of the Structure and Elasticities of Mexican Imports in the Period 1961-1969", *Journal of Development Economics*, June 1982, 10(3), pp. 297-311.

Salas, Javier, "Estimacion de la Funcion de Importaciones para Mexico", *El Trimestre Economico*, April-June 1982, 49(194), pp. 295-335.

Salas, Javier, "Estimacion de la Funcion de Importaciones para Mexico: Una Revision", *El Trimestre Economico*, October-December, 1988, 55(220), pp. 819-846.

Salehi-Isfahani, Djavad, "Oil Exports, Real Exchnge Rate Appreciation and Demand for Imports in Nigeria", *Economic Development and Cultural Change*, April 1989, 37(3), pp. 495-512.

Sarmad, Khwaja, "The Functional Form of the Aggregate Import Demand Equation: Evidence from Developing Countries", *Pakistan Development Review*, Autumn 1988, 27(3), pp. 309-315.

Sarmad, Khwaja, "The Determinants of Import Demand in Pakistan", *World Development*, October 1989, 17(10), pp. 1619-1625.

Sarmad, Khwaja and Riaz Mahmood, "Price and Income Elasticities of Consumer Goods Imports of Pakistan", *Pakistan Development Review*, Autumn-Winter 1985, 24(3/4), pp. 453-460.

Sarmad, Khwaja and Riaz Mahmood, "Disaggregated Import Demand Functions for Pakistan", *Pakistan Development Review*, Spring 1987, 26(1), pp. 71-80.

Sawyer, W. Charles and Richard L. Sprinkle, "An Examination of U.S. Imports and Exports of Finished Manufactures", *Rivista Internazionale di Scienze Economiche e Commerciali*, March 1997, 44(1), pp. 139-148.

Sazanami, Y. and A. Matsumura, "Income and Price Elasticities in U.S.-Japan Bilateral Trade", *Keio Economic Studies*, 1985, 22(1), pp. 47-56.

Shabbir, Tayyeb and Riaz, Mahmood, "Structural Change in the Import Demand Function for Pakistan", *Pakistan Development Review*, Winter 1991, 30(4), pp. 1159-1166.

Shiells, Clinton R., *A Disaggregated Empirical Analysis of U.S. Import Demand, 1962-1981*, Ann Arbor: University of Michigan, 1985.

Shiells, Clinton R., "Errors in Import-Demand Estimates Based Upon Unit-Value Indexes", *Review of Economics and Statistics*, May 1991, 73(2), pp. 378-382.

Shiells, Clinton R. and K. A. Reinert, "Armington Models and Terms-of-Trade Effects: Some Econometric Evidence for North America", *Canadian Journal of Economics*, May 1993, 26(2), pp. 299-316.

Shiells, Clinton R., Robert M. Stern, and Alan V. Deardorff, "Estimates of the Elasticities of Substitution between Imports and Home Goods for the United States", *Weltwirtschaftliches Archiv*, 1986, 122(3), pp. 497-519.

Smit, B. W., "The Variability of the Rand and South African Exports", *Journal for Studies in Economics and Econometrics*, June 1991, 15(2), pp. 19-29.

Stern, Robert M., Christopher F. Baum, and Mark N. Greene, "Evidence on Structural Change in the Demand for Aggregate U.S. Imports and Exports", *Journal of Political Economy*, February 1979, 87(1), pp. 179-192.

Stern, Robert M., J. Francis, and Bruce Schumacher, *Price Elasticities in International Trade*, London: Basingstoke, 1976.

Sundararajan, S. and L. M. Bhole, "Functional Form of the Import Demand Function", *Margin*, April-June 1989, 21(3), pp. 52-65.

Tansel, Aysit and Subidey Togan, "Price and Income Effects in Turkish Foreign Trade", *Weltwirtschaftliches Archiv*, 1987, 123(3), pp. 521-534.

Tegene, Abebayehu, "On the Effects of Relative Prices and Effective Exchange Rates on Trade Flows of LDCs", *Applied Economics*, November 1989, 21(11), pp. 1447-1463.

Tegene, Abebayehu, "The Supply and Demand for Exports in Some African Countries: A Simultaneous Equation Model", *Journal of Quantitative Economics*, July 1990, 6(2), pp. 395-410.

Thursby, Jerry G. and Marie Thursby, "How Reliable are Simple, Single-Equation Specifications of Import Demand?", *Review of Economics and Statistics*, February 1984, 66(1), pp. 120-128.

Truett, Dale B. and Lila J. Truett, "Nonprimary Exports of African LDCs: Have Trade Preferences Helped?", *Journal of Developing Areas*, July 1992, 26(4), pp. 457-473.

Umo, Joe U., "Import Demand and Export Supply Elasticities for African Countries: A Comparative Analysis", *Journal of Business and Social Studies*, 1981, 5, pp. 43-54.

Umo, Joe U., "An Analysis of Nigeria's Trade with Special Reference to Import Demand", in *Trade and Development in Sub-Saharan Africa*, Jonathan H. Frimpong-Anash, S. M. Ravi Kanbur, and Peter Svedberg, eds., New York: Manchester University Press, 1991, pp. 262-280.

Urbain, Jean-Pierre, "Error Correction Models for Aggregate Imports: The Case of Two Small and Open Economies", in *International Trade Modelling*, M. G. Dagenais and P-A. Muet, eds., London: Chipman and Hall, 1992, pp. 237-278.

Urbain, Jean-Pierre, "Japanese Import Behavior and Cointegration: A Comment", *Journal of Policy Modeling*, December 1996, 18(6), pp. 583-601.

Volker, Paul A., "On the U.S. Import Demand Function: A Comment", *Journal of Political Economy*, December 1982, 90(6), pp. 1295-1299.

Warner, Dennis and Mordechai E. Kreinin, "Determinants of International Trade Flows", *Review of Economics and Statistics*, February 1983, 65(1), pp. 96-104.

Weisskoff, R., "Trade, Protection, and Import Elasticities for Brazil", *Review of Economics and Statistics*, February 1979, 51(1), pp. 58-66.

Welsch, Heinz, "An Aggregate Import Demand Model for Long-term Projections", *Jahrbucher fur Nationalokonomie und Statistik*, July 1987, 203(4), pp. 372-389.

Wilde, L.C., L. Cornell, V. Sorenson, and J. Black, *World Grain Trade: An Evaluation of Factors Affecting Net Import Demand for Wheat and Coarse Grains by Selected Countries*, Michigan State University, 1986.

Wilkinson, Jenny, "Explaining Australia's Imports", *Economic Record*, June 1992, 68(201), pp. 151-164.

Wilson, John F. and Wendy E. Takacs, "Differential Responses to Price and Exchange Rate Influences in the Foreign Trade of Selected Industrial Countries" *Review of Economics and Statistics*, April 1979, 61(2), pp. 267-279.

Witte, W. E., "The Lagged Adjustment of Canadian Exports to Prices and Foreign Activity, 1973-1978", *Review of Economics and Statistics*, May 1981, 63(2), pp. 303-307.

Wu, Xi-Ling, "Testing the Trade Impact of Institutional Changes: A Switching Regression Analysis of the EC s Soybean Imports", *European Review of Agricultural Economics*, 1992, 19(3), pp. 301-312.

Yadav, Gopal, "A Quarterly Model of the Canadian Demand for Imports 1956-72", *Canadian Journal of Economics*, August 1975, 8(3), pp. 410-422.

Yadav, Gopal, "Variable Elasticities and Non-Price Rationing in the Import Demand Function of Canada, 1956:1-1973:4", *Canadian Journal of Economics*, November 1977, 10(4), pp. 702-712.

Yang, Bong M. "The Supply and Demand for Exports for Industrialized Countries: A Disequilibrium Analysis", *Applied Economics*, 1987, 19(9), pp. 1137-1148.

Zeitz, Joachim, "The Impacts of Oil Shocks and Exchange Rate Changes on Import Demand Elasticities", *Weltwirtschaftliches Archiv*, 1992, 128(2), pp. 237-247.

Zeitz, Joachim and D. K. Pemberton, "Parameter Instability in Aggregate U.S. Import Demand Functions", *Journal of International Money and Finance*, December 1993, 12(6), pp. 654-667.

Zilberfarb, Ben-Zion, "Domestic Demand Pressure, Relative Prices, and the Exports Supply Equation-More Empirical Evidence", *Economica*, November 1980, 47(108), pp. 443-450.

Zini, Alvaro A., "Funcoes de Exportacao e de Importacao para o Brasil", *Pesquisa e Planejamento Economico*, December 1988, 18(3), pp. 615-661.

Zonzilos, Nicholas G., "Modelling Imports When Variables are Stochastically Trending", *Greek Economic Review*, December 1991, 13(2), pp. 269-286.

For Product Safety Concerns and Information please contact our EU representative GPSR@taylorandfrancis.com Taylor & Francis Verlag GmbH, Kaufingerstraße 24, 80331 München, Germany

Printed and bound by CPI Group (UK) Ltd, Croydon, CR0 4YY

08/05/2025

01864362-0003